on track ...

The Rolling Stones

every album, every song
1963-1980

Steve Pilkington

Sonicbond Publishing Limited
www.sonicbondpublishing.co.uk
Email: info@sonicbondpublishing.co.uk

First Published in the United Kingdom 2019
First Published in the United States 2019

British Library Cataloguing in Publication Data:
A Catalogue record for this book is available from the British Library

ISBN 978-1-78952-017-0

Typset in ITC Garamond & Berthold Akzidenz Grotesk
Printed and bound in England

Graphic design and typesetting: Full Moon Media

on track ...

The Rolling Stones

every album, every song
1963-1980

Steve Pilkington

sonicbondpublishing.co.uk

Acknowledgements

Thanks to Stephen Lambe, for commissioning the book despite having read my earlier ones! Janet for patience, opinions, support when I threatened to destroy my Stones collection and keeping the dogs out of the way. Finally, thanks to all of those people who have done research before me – I believe 'Standing on the shoulders of giants' is the apt phrase.

Huge thanks to Matt Lee, Curt Angeledes, Gudbjorg Ogmundsdottir and Glenn Michael Schneiderfor photo contributions.

Thanks of course, everyone who has appeared on a Stones recording over the years, either as a core band member or as one of the many guest musicians. Were it not for them, etc etc...

And finally, big thanks to anyone who has bought this, or any of my books. I truly hope you find it informative and/or entertaining!

on track ...
The Rolling Stones
1963-1980

Contents

Introduction

In the minds of most people who were around in the early 1960s, the Rolling Stones were inextricably linked to their image as the 'dark side' to the clean-cut Beatles. Fans in those early days tended to gravitate to either the Beatles or Stones camp, and the Stones were always the more rebellious, 'dangerous' option. The first seeds of the band were sown in October 1961 when a chance meeting between Keith Richards and Mick Jagger on Dartford Railway Station in Kent saw them discover a shared musical interest over the Muddy Waters and Chuck Berry albums Jagger was carrying with him. In fact, the pair had known each other a decade earlier at school, but their paths had very much diverged with Jagger now attending the London School of Economics.

During the '50s Jagger had started a rudimentary band with guitarist Dick Taylor, who became the original Stones bassist alongside Jagger and Richards, with early bandleader Brian Jones and keyboard player Ian Stewart, before leaving in November 1962 to be replaced by Bill Wyman. He soon formed the Pretty Things, whose image ironically made the Stones appear like well-behaved boys next door! The arrival of Charlie Watts late in 1962 saw the first 'classic' line-up in place, though Stewart, who was older than the rest and frankly looked like their slightly uncomfortable uncle, left the official line-up in 1962 to continue as tour manager, and also some-time keyboardist for a long period afterwards.

Initially concentrating on blues and R&B covers, the band soon started recording original material – a move which was opposed by the purist Jones. This brought them enormous success with a string of huge hit singles and increasingly successful albums throughout the '60s, which saw them incorporating rock, blues, psychedelia and country elements into a sound uniquely their own. In 1969, Jones officially departed the band, having been more and more peripheral owing to his own personal demons over the previous couple of years. He was immediately replaced by Mick Taylor, whose first show with the band was the famous Hyde Park free concert which saw Jagger release butterflies and recite poetry by Shelley in remembrance of Jones who had drowned in his swimming pool a month after leaving the band. Taylor's five year spell in the band produced some of the band's most enduring music, taking in the run of albums from *Let It Bleed* through to *It's Only Rock 'n' Roll* in 1974, and saw the only time in the band's career that they utilised a true technical virtuoso as opposed to their otherwise loose, ragged but thrilling chemistry.

On Taylor's departure in 1974, Faces guitarist Ron Wood joined, forming a partnership with Richards which continues to the present day – although he is still regarded by many as the 'new boy'! Further key recordings such as *Black and Blue* and *Some Girls* saw out the decade in some style, if not as great as what had gone before, but as the 1980s developed so the band's influence and status declined; though remaining enormously popular they began to be regarded more and more as 'elder statesmen' as opposed to the hungry rebels who had stalked the '60s and '70s. It is, therefore, the period from 1963 to 1980 which will be covered in this book, examining how the band developed and evolved during the crucible of those initial years, and how that led them to be afforded the unofficial accolade of 'the greatest rock and roll band in the world'.

Ladies and gentlemen, The Rolling Stones!

The Rolling Stones.
US Title: England's Newest Hit Makers (1964)

Personnel:
Mick Jagger: vocals, harmonica
Keith Richards: guitar, vocals
Brian Jones: guitar, harmonica, vocals
Bill Wyman: bass guitar, vocals
Charlie Watts: drums and percussion
With
Ian Stewart: piano, organ
Gene Pitney: piano
Phil Spector: maracas

Record Label: Decca (UK), London (US)
Recorded: Jan-Feb 1964, produced by Eric Easton and Andrew Loog Oldham
UK release date: April 1964. US release date: May 1964
Highest chart places: UK: 1, USA: 11
Running time: UK: 33:24 US: 31:05
The US track listing substituted the hit single 'Not Fade Away' for the song 'Mona'. This is covered at the end of this section.

Album Facts:

By the time the Stones entered Regent Studios in London to record their debut album they had already had a small taste of success via the Top 5 single 'Not Fade Away', so they were riding high on a wave of self-belief. The album itself was recorded in very basic fashion on a two-track Revox, so there was very little scope for embellishment beyond the most rudimentary of overdubs and everything you hear is more or less as it was played at the time. This factor, combined with the band's cocksure arrogance and belief in their own abilities, resulted in an album which gets out of the starting blocks quickly and never lets up. It's dated now, naturally – but in comparison to many of the albums churned out by 'beat groups' of the time, with a host of B-sides and filler tracks padding them out, it's a beacon of excitement and bravado. One thing which is clear from the way the instrumentation is pushed forward as strongly as the vocals is that the band, even at this stage, regarded themselves as musicians first and foremost, rather than as pop stars.

The US release of the album included 'Not Fade Away' at the expense of 'Mona' – though it is difficult to see why it was necessary to drop that track, as the change left the first side of the US release at only 13 minutes and 42 seconds; extremely short, even for the time.

Album Cover:

By the time of this album's release, after three singles and an EP of covers called *The Rolling Stones EP* (none of those EP tracks are particularly noteworthy), the fledgling Stones had already cultivated a highly visual image as 'rebels', who parents across the land feared would come and steal their daughters away, which by turn heightened the cleaner-cut allure of the Beatles, whose 'long-haired' early demeanour quickly became almost cuddly by comparison. Manager Andrew Loog Oldham, a shrewd individual, knew this only too well, and he traded on it in a risky move whereby the name of the band was left off the front cover of the album entirely, with the Decca logo the only writing visible. Instead, all the attention was focused on the picture – a band photo as was the norm, but a much darker example of that form, with the band side-on and looking over their shoulders in surly fashion. At a time when marketing was king in terms of album design, and most LPs still featured the tracks on the front as well as the band name and title, this was unheard of, but a decision that paid off spectacularly as the album hit the Number One spot in the UK album charts.

In the USA the band had no such established image, so the American release contained not only the band name but also the cringe-inducing tag line 'England's Newest Hit Makers', which has gone on over the years to become the de facto accepted title of the album over there – heaven knows why! Even in England, it has to be said, the record company's bravery would only stretch so far, and the rear of the album was emblazoned with the band name in the biggest possible font, along with captioned photos of the five members. Brief sleeve notes by Oldham featured alongside the track listing and credits. One noteworthy point here is that Keith was known as 'Keith Richard' at this time, dropping the final 'S' from his surname for professional purposes. This was the case for most of the scope of this book, and he has been credited deliberately as 'Richards' throughout, as he generally is retrospectively these days.

'Route 66' (Troup)

Opening the album is this R&B standard which many people mistakenly assume to be written by Chuck Berry, who had recorded it in 1961. It was in actual fact written by George Troup in 1946 and tells the story of a real-life road trip he made with his wife Christine, heading to Hollywood with the intention of making it as a songwriter. In fact, the original title was to be 'US 40', after the road of that name, before Christine came up with the immortal line 'get your kicks on Route 66'. The first recording of the song was Nat King Cole's excellent take in 1946, but bizarrely – given the nature of versions such as this one – it was a US hit in that same year for Bing Crosby with The Andrews Sisters! That one isn't a particularly thrilling rendition by the way.

The Stones rendition holds its own against any other recorded version, especially of the time, and still sounds good today. Well chosen as the album opener, Jagger excels with the vocal while the opening of the instrumental break is infused with thrilling momentum. A statement of intent, for sure.

'I Just Want to Make Love to You' (Dixon)

Next up is this Willie Dixon standard, written in 1964. The Stones attack the song with a sort of zealous relish here, ramping up the tempo and making the track a world away from Muddy Waters' slow blues version. The middle eight is particularly exciting, but the whole track perfectly illustrates the chasm which existed between the Beatles and the Stones at this time. The Beatles wanted to hold your hand and send you all their loving – Jagger just sounds like he has one thing on his mind, and one way or another he's going to get it. For 1964, this was pure sex in musical form. And you could dance to it.

'Honest I Do' (Reed)

Written by Jimmy Reed, this two-minute mid-tempo blues shuffle is arguably one of the less celebrated tracks from the album. Nevertheless, there is much to recommend it, from Jones' urgent harmonica – contrasting with the laid-back, easy feel of the rest of the band – to Jagger's nonchalant delivery. It seems unremarkable now, but at the time blues was extremely uncommon in the mainstream in such an 'unsweetened' form, and nobody was doing it better than the Stones.

'Mona (I Need You Baby)' (McDaniel)

Written by Elias McDaniel, aka Bo Diddley, this originally saw the light of day as the B-side to his self-referential 'Hey! Bo Diddley' single in 1957. In truth, this is a big improvement on the rather dry Diddley original, with the heavily echoed guitar courtesy of Brian Jones giving the song a depth and full sound lacking from the original. The song was allegedly a big influence on Buddy Holly when he wrote 'Not Fade Away', and in retrospect, the similarity between the two songs could well have been the reason behind the decision to drop this track from the US release. Once again, the Stones take on a cover from a revered influence and beat them at their own game...

'Now I've Got A Witness (Like Uncle Phil And Uncle Gene)' (Nanker Phelge)

Some explanation is required here around the title and credit for this throwaway instrumental. The dedication to uncles Phil and Gene refer to Phil Spector and Gene Pitney, who are both claimed to have contributed as guests on the following track, 'Little by Little'. As for the writing credit, 'Nanker Phelge' was a pseudonym used in the early days of the band for any tracks which were deemed as co-writes by the whole band, and all members would receive royalty payments on those songs. The term 'Nanker' refers to a somewhat hideous face often pulled by the band (and Jones especially), which involved simultaneously pulling down the underside of the eyes and pushing up the nose. The 'Phelge' part also has its roots in unpleasantness, as it refers to a flatmate of the band by the name of Jimmy Phelge, who Keith would describe as a 'revolting' individual. Apologies to Mr Phelge if that description was less than accurate!

As for the track itself, it is a simple walking blues, enjoyable if insubstantial. Driven by Jones' enthusiastic harmonica, the lead guitar break on this, brief as it is, comes courtesy of Keith.

'Little by Little' (Nanker Phelge, Spector)

Co-credited to Phil Spector alongside the group 'Nanker Phelge' writing credit, Gene Pitney allegedly plays piano on this track (though some maintain it is actually all Ian Stewart on the ivories), with Spector himself providing the somewhat less technically demanding maracas. The track is probably the weakest on the first side of the record, being another twelve-bar outing which, while taken at quite a sprightly pace, is nevertheless little more than generic R&B which the band could probably churn out in their sleep. Jagger takes over the harmonica on this one, while Richards provides the lead guitar in the instrumental break – but it isn't really his finest hour.

'I'm A King Bee' (Moore)

The second side of the vinyl opens with this piece of churning swamp-blues courtesy of James Moore – better known as Slim Harpo. With Jagger on harmonica duty again as Jones busies himself with some slide guitar, the band stick pretty closely to the original Harpo arrangement as recorded on his 1957 original – right down to Bill Wyman's insistent bassline – but if anything, they nail down the groove even tighter. The longer the song progresses, the more the listener gets sucked into the hypnotic nature of the instrumental work, and it is a real testament to how good a band the Stones were, even at this early stage in their career. Jagger has since been quoted as giving his opinion that it was pointless for people to listen to them doing this when they could simply listen to Slim Harpo doing it, but he is being far too self-critical.

'Carol' (Berry)

Ah, the album could never go by without a Chuck Berry song, so in thrall were Jagger and Richards in particular to his influence at the time. The song itself is unremarkable, being essentially 'Johnny B Goode' with a new haircut, but the way the Stones attack it is revelatory. So tight is the playing here that a cigarette paper could not have been put between the musicians, and the sound remains vital some 55 years after the fact. Indeed, a decade later, bands such as Dr Feelgood and Eddie and the Hot Rods would gleefully run with the template laid down by this track. Essential.

'Tell Me (You're Coming Back)' (Jagger, Richards)

The only Jagger/Richards song on the record – and actually the first one the band had recorded themselves, though Gene Pitney had already recorded a song they wrote called 'My Only Girl', which he retitled as 'That Girl Belongs to Yesterday'. 'Tell Me' is an excellent song, and far removed from the frantic R&B flailing of the rest of the material, good as it is. Quite acoustic-based in construction, the verses show Jagger in reflective mood against some plangent guitars, while the chorus ramps up the pace and the energy level. It's a remarkably sophisticated pop song given their lack of compositional experience at this time.

'Can I Get A Witness' (Holland, Dozier, Holland)

Written by the redoubtable Motown songwriting team, and released a year earlier as a single by Marvin Gaye, the Stones' rendition removed all of the soulful sharp-suited Motown identifiers from the song and basically rebranded it as 100% pure Stones R&B. Driven along by Ian Stewart's pumping barrelhouse piano, this is another successful reinterpretation, and fairly motors along. The basic progression was effectively reworked for the 'Now I've Got A Witness' track on the previous side. As an example of how influential this stuff could be even across genres, check out the Emerson Lake and Palmer song 'Tiger In A Spotlight', and see just how much it owes to this track.

'You Can Make It If You Try' (Jarrett)

Ah well, no album can be perfect! Nearing the end of the record comes this pedestrian reworking of an unremarkable song, originally written by Ted Jarrett for Gene Allison. Generic blues fare, this is in effect filling up two minutes of the album.

'Walking the Dog' (Thomas)

Closing the album is this much-covered Rufus Thomas song, and the Stones clearly have fun with it, with Jagger getting into the party spirit with dog whistles and calls. A brief instrumental break showcases Jones, but this is Jagger's show more than anyone else. Not exactly a substantial classic of any great note, but an enjoyable way to finish the album for sure.

Related Songs:

'Come On' (Berry)

The very first Stones single, recorded at Olympic Studios in May 1963, it was released in June that year. It reworks the original somewhat feeble Berry arrangement substantially, tighter and taken in a far more rocking manner, but it is not especially exciting and, at one minute and 45 seconds, seems rushed to say the least! Promising, but they could and would do better.

'I Want to Be Loved' (Dixon)

The B-side to 'Come On', this Willie Dixon cover is essentially more of the same. Tight, energetic but somehow unremarkable, Jones' harmonica is too prevalent on this while Jagger sounds as if he is trying to affect a different vocal delivery which does him no favours.

'I Wanna Be Your Man' (Lennon, McCartney)

Well, I bet nobody saw this one coming! As the press and media generally were falling over themselves to initiate a Beatles v Stones rivalry, the Stones score a number 12 hit in November 1963 with, what else, a Lennon/McCartney composition! Not only that, but it appeared before the Beatles' own version, on the *With the Beatles* LP. In truth, it isn't the most sophisticated piece of songcraft John and Paul would ever produce, but it drives along quite satisfactorily. Which version you prefer largely depends which band you prefer at this stage of their development – the Stones take is far harder, grittier and rawer, with some aggressive lead guitar work from Jones and a fabulous bassline from the underrated Wyman, whereas the Beatles' own recording is smoother and slicker.

'Stoned' (Nanker Phelge)

Just when you were wondering whether the Stones were really any different to those 'cuddly moptops', here comes a B-side which may back a Beatles composition but would never have appeared on a Beatles recording! Musically a rather meandering instrumental cut from the 'Green Onions' cloth, the band push the envelope with Jagger's occasional, heavily echoed, interjections of 'Stoned ... Outta mah mind ... Where am I at?', leaving the listener in little doubt that this was not named after the band. An early statement of their contempt for authority and censorship, the song was soon withdrawn in the US, not getting an official release until it was included on a 1989 compilation. Early pressings had the title misspelt as 'Stones', which may illustrate the naiveté of the record company...

'Not Fade Away (Holly, Petty)

The band's first top ten hit arrived with this sprightly interpretation of the Buddy Holly song, which sees our bespectacled hero himself channelling Bo Diddley. Which means you know exactly what it's going to sound like. Yep, that rhythm again. It's well enough done, but the band had yet to find their own voice. 'Little by Little' adorns the flip side.

'It's All Over Now' (Womack, Womack)

Now, this is where it all started to fall into place, as the Stones scored their first number one hit with the first single to come out after the debut album. The record is a cover of a song by the Valentinos, featuring Bobby Womack, but is revamps the somewhat jaunty soul of the original in every possible way. Opening with a sonorous, slow-paced guitar figure, the listener is wrong-footed until the first verse comes in over the almost country-influenced jangle of the guitars. The tale of a no-good cheating woman getting her comeuppance is delivered much better by Jagger than by Womack, and the chorus becomes an irresistible hook due largely to the ringing power-chords behind it. A great single, it was recorded at Chess Studios in Chicago, along with five tracks for an EP entitled *5x5* (of which more below).

'Good Times, Bad Times' (Jagger, Richards)

The B-side to 'It's All Over Now', recorded a few weeks earlier in London, proves that sometimes B-sides were far from undiscovered classics – indeed, as this effort shows, sometimes they could be weak-kneed blues drones accompanied by frantically scrubbed acoustic guitars and a wholly unconvincing vocal. Nobody really needs this.

'Empty Heart' (Nanker Phelge)

One of the two originals on the *5x5* EP (alongside decent enough covers of 'If She Needs Me', 'Confessin' The Blues' and, perhaps the highlight, Chuck Berry's 'Around and Around') cruises along on a fractured, choppy rhythm which makes the best of what is a slightly mediocre song

'2120 South Michigan Avenue' (Nanker Phelge)

The title of this self-penned instrumental was the Stones' way of immortalising their visit to Chess Records, a Mecca of sorts to any blues-loving British youngster of the time, and where they were actually greeted by Muddy Waters himself. The title is, of course, the address of the studio in Chicago. The song developed from the opening insistent bass riff initiated by Wyman, as the rest of the band jumped in and jammed on it. Ian Stewart plays some very effective organ here, and overall it is an excellent, and rather infectious, piece. There was a longer version which eventually surfaced on a CD issue of the US album *12x5* – the story often circulated was that it was edited due to contractual reasons as Muddy Waters picked up a guitar and joined in, but it is more likely to have simply been to fit it onto the five-song 7" EP in the first place.

'Little Red Rooster' (Dixon)

After the success of 'It's All Over Now', everyone expected the band to follow up with a similarly radio-friendly single. They failed to reckon on the contrary streak of the Stones, however, as they committed what many believed to be commercial suicide by putting out the innuendo-laden pure blues of Willie Dixon's 'Little Red Rooster'. Remarkably, however, this tactic paid off as, somehow, the sound of Jagger lamenting the fact that his little red rooster is 'too lame to crow today' (and he clearly wasn't referring to fatigued wildfowl down on the farm) to the accompaniment of a harmonica-laden slow 12-bar, headed straight to the top of the singles chart, albeit for just one week. Clearly, by now, momentum was gathering behind the band. This song was the last cover version to be released as a single by the Stones in the UK until the 1980s.

12x5 (1964) – *US Only Release*

Personnel:
Mick Jagger: vocals, harmonica
Keith Richards: guitar, vocals
Brian Jones: guitar, harmonica, vocals
Bill Wyman: bass guitar, vocals
Charlie Watts: drums and percussion
With
Ian Stewart: piano

Record Label: London (US)
Recorded: Feb-Sept 1964, produced by Andrew Loog Oldham
US release date: October 1964
Highest chart places: US: 3
Running time: 30:50

This US-only album contained the five tracks from the *5x5* EP plus other singles and UK-issued tracks. This is discussed further in the section covering *The Rolling Stones No 2*

'Around And Around' (Chuck Berry)

An excellent cover of the Berry track, this sprightly version was perhaps the highlight of *5x5*.

'Confessin' The Blues' (McShann / Brown)

This 1941 track by Walter Brown and Jay McShann, from the EP, is a relatively undistinguished offering, if well played.

'Empty Heart'

(see section *The Rolling Stones*, Related Songs)

'Time Is On My Side'

(See section *The Rolling Stones No 2*)

'Good Times, Bad Times'

(see section *The Rolling Stones*, Related Songs)

'It's All Over Now'

(see section *The Rolling Stones*, Related Songs)

'2120 South Michigan Avenue'

(see section *The Rolling Stones*, Related Songs)

'Under The Boardwalk'

(see section *The Rolling Stones No 2*)

'Congratulations'

(see section *The Rolling Stones No 2*, Related Songs)

'Grown Up Wrong'

(see section *The Rolling Stones No 2*)

'If You Need Me' (Bateman, Pickett)

The last of the three covers on the *5x5* EP, this version of the 1962 Wilson Pickett song, also recorded by Solomon Burke, again shows the band in rather formative mode, not yet quite making the song their own

'Susie-Q'

(see section *The Rolling Stones No 2*)

The Rolling Stones No 2 (1965)

Personnel:
Mick Jagger: vocals, harmonica
Keith Richards: guitar, vocals
Brian Jones: guitar, vocals
Bill Wyman: bass guitar, vocals
Charlie Watts: drums and percussion
With
Ian Stewart: piano, organ
Jack Nitzsche: piano

Record Label: Decca (UK)
Recorded: June, Sept, Nov 1964, produced by Andrew Loog Oldham
UK release date: January 1965. US release date: No release
Highest chart places: UK: 1
Running time: 36:58

Album Facts:

Things were getting complicated with the Stones releases on opposite sides of the Atlantic. By the time this second album appeared in the UK in early 1965, a US album called *12x5* had already appeared. Taking its title from the *5x5* EP, it unsurprisingly contained the tracks from that record, together with some which would appear on this official sophomore effort and a few other odds and ends from single releases. Shortly AFTER this album's release, a third US album appeared entitled *The Rolling Stones Now!*, containing the remainder of these songs which hadn't appeared on *12x5* together with some more offcuts. Confused? You're not alone. If the EP had been released as it was in the US, the *12x5* album would likely have never appeared, but the US record label, London Records, declined to do so as they claimed EPs were not popular in the American market. If they had done so then it is possible that the second Stones album would have had the same title and basic tracklisting everywhere, and both completist collectors and authors of books such as this could have had an easier time of it! For consistency, throughout this book, the UK albums will be treated as the official releases.

The album (this time produced by Oldham alone) followed the same general template and sound palette as the debut – albeit leaning toward a more soul-influenced R&B flavour – though there were three Jagger/Richards originals this time out. There could, and probably should, have been more, but it would seem that they were still not entirely confident in their own songwriting. That would come soon. Very soon.

Album Cover:

Just to confuse everyone still further, the photograph used for the album cover is the same one used on that pesky *12x5* album a short time earlier. Oldham again insisted on the front cover to the UK album appearing with no title or band name on it, and once again it paid off as the record topped the UK chart. The photo this time out was if anything even less glamorous than the one on the debut, as the band gaze out with expressions straight from a prison movie. Jagger looks hungover or stoned, Richards appears to be gazing into some sort of existential abyss, while Charlie Watts resembles a psychotic hit-man who thoroughly enjoys his work. This wasn't With the Beatles, that's for sure. The rear cover, like the debut, had sleeve notes by Oldham along with monochrome band photos and the track list in block lettering.

'Everybody Needs Somebody to Love' (Burke, Berns, Wexler)

The opening track on the album sees the band dive head first into the soul arena with this spirited cover of a Solomon Burke single from the previous year. The band sound confident and sure of themselves straight away, but it must be said that, clocking in at a (long for the time) five minutes it does begin to wear out its welcome. There are live recordings (and in particular a US TV appearance) from the time showing this to be much better in live performance. A different, and shorter, version of the track was included on the US album *The Rolling Stones Now!*, but this turned out to be an earlier take which was used in error.

'Down Home Girl' (Leiber, Butler)

Another cover, as the band tackle this swampy blues grind first released a year earlier by US singer Alvin 'Shine' Robinson. A tale of lust and lechery with a farm girl, Jagger is at his lascivious best here as he rolls his tongue around such lines as 'Every time I kiss you girl, it tastes like pork and beans' (imagine the Beatles doing that one). The band take the song down to make it darker and more menacing, with guitar replacing the horn riff in the original and use of the harmonica bringing out the blues still more. This is another of those examples of the Stones hitting a groove and just sitting there as they make it their own. A very accomplished track which should really be better known.

'You Can't Catch Me' (Berry)

A Chuck Berry cover here, but not an expected or obvious one, as they take on this single from 1956, with the everyday tale of a guy racing in a fast car before it sprouts wings and he takes off. In truth, there's a reason why it isn't one of Berry's greatest hits, as it is somewhat repetitive, and the Stones follow the original arrangement quite faithfully, especially Jagger's vocal. The song was also covered by John Lennon on his 1975 album *Rock and Roll*, though the reason behind that is somewhat more interesting, as he was sued for plagiarism of this in the Beatles track 'Come Together', and the settlement included an agreement to cover the song.

'Time Is on My Side' (Meade)

One of the more well-known of the early Stones songs, this is one which many people assume was an original composition but it was actually written by US songwriter Jerry Ragovoy, under the pseudonym of Norman Meade for no discernible reason. First recorded by jazz trombonist Kai Wilding in 1963, it had extra words added by Jimmy Norman (originally, 'Time is on my side' and 'You'll come running back' were the only lyrics!) before being covered by soul singer Irma Thomas and the Stones. The song was originally included on the US *12x5* album, and also released as a US single, but the later version on this album is the more common one. The easiest way to immediately differentiate between the two is that the earlier US version features an organ intro, while the UK version has a guitar in its place.

'What A Shame' (Jagger, Richards)

The first of three Jagger / Richards compositions on the album, sadly this one really doesn't cut the mustard in any shape or form. A derivative leaden-footed 12-bar blues, it tries to liven up its plodding substance by persistent guitar and harmonica accompaniment, but both of these are as unremarkable as the song itself. Never performed live, it's easy to see why. Based on this, their rapid ascent to supremely accomplished songwriters seems all the more remarkable.

'Grown Up Wrong' (Jagger, Richards)

Another original closing the vinyl first side, this brief two-minute song is slightly better than 'What A Shame', having much more energy and at least something of a spring in its step, but let's not kid ourselves here, this is still pretty lean songwriting fare.

'Down the Road Apiece' (Raye)

Another song which has been covered by acts as diverse as Chuck Berry and Foghat, this driving boogie-woogie number is another one written way back – in fact dating back as far as 1940 when it was first recorded by the Will Bradley Trio, who must rank as one of the oddest named recording acts in history since, firstly, there were four of them and, secondly, they did not include Will Bradley (though they did include the song's composer, Don Raye). When first written, the song referenced members of the original band in the lyric 'The drummer man's a guy they call "Eight Beat Mack" / And you remember Doc and ol' "Beat Me Daddy" Slack', which had them playing in the venue which was 'down the road apiece'. These references evolved over the years until Chuck Berry referenced a drummer called 'Johnny McCoy', who was oddly also 'that rubber-legged boy'. When the Stones recorded their version, the drummer was 'Charlie McCoy', which is presumably a nod to Charlie Watts. It's an excellent track, and a standout on the album, possessing an unstoppable locomotive energy and propelled along by Ian Stewarts exceptional boogie piano. The early Stones at their best.

'Under the Boardwalk' (Resnick, Young)

Everyone knows this Drifters song, of course (a 1964 hit which has become a standard), and it is a little odd to hear the Stones attempting it, in this take which first appeared on *12x5*. They take it in a slightly Spanish-sounding fashion, with acoustic guitars and hand-held percussion in strong evidence. In truth, it doesn't really work. This is partly because of its over-familiarity in its Drifters guise, but it also sees the Stones being pushed a little too awkwardly into the Soul box. Mind you, still better than Bruce Willis covering it...

'I Can't Be Satisfied' (Waters)

Ah, here we have Muddy Waters, as the Stones pay homage to one of their key blues influences. He needn't have worried about being outclassed exactly, as this take is oddly anaemic. Brian Jones contributes some nice slide guitar, but it sounds as if he is recording it at the bottom of a well, and there have been shire horses whose hooves sound more exciting than Watts' drums on here. Avoid this.

'Pain in My Heart' (Toussaint)

Another interesting one here. Written by prolific songwriter and producer Allen Toussaint (under the pseudonym Naomi Neville, for no obvious reason) and first recorded in 1963 by Irma Thomas, it was originally called 'Ruler of My Heart'. In 1964 Otis Redding substantially reworked the song under the title 'Pain in My Heart'. After a lawsuit, Redding's label Stax Records agreed to credit the song to Toussaint, but although they honoured that credit the Stones took Redding's arrangement as their template. Again it is unexceptional, but certainly an improvement over the two songs preceding it.

'Off the Hook' (Jagger, Richards)

The third and final Jagger / Richards song on the album, and thankfully it is the best of the three. A simple but entertaining tale of Jagger getting increasingly frustrated about his 'baby' being engaged when he tries to phone her, worrying about all the possible reasons, before finally responding by leaving his own phone off the hook is delivered in quite infectious and lively fashion – at least, after a dreadful guitar intro proves a thankful false start. The chorus is somewhat repetitive, to say the least, but promise is certainly there.

'Susie-Q' (Hawkins, Lewis, Broadwater)

A rather brief conclusion to the album, this run-through of the Dale Hawkins rockabilly song comes in at a rather paltry one minute and 50 seconds. It's reasonable for what it is but is utterly eclipsed by the definitive version of the song recorded later in the decade by Creedence Clearwater Revival. Hawkins actually wrote the song himself, but record company owner Stan Lewis and

Eleanor Broadwater (wife of US DJ Gene Nobles) were given credits in order to provide them with a share of the royalties.

Related Songs:

'Congratulations' (Jagger, Richards)

The B-side to the US single 'Time Is On My Side', this track did not get an official release in the UK. It's an interesting early example, being delivered in bitingly sarcastic fashion to the subject who has broken another heart. 'Congratulations', Jagger informs him, 'You've done it again!'. Quite dark and introspective sounding for the time.

'The Last Time' (Jagger, Richards)

Now, where in the world did this come from? Released as a single only a month or so following the album, the difference between this song and the self-penned album efforts is astonishing. From rather derivative and tentative bluesy numbers the Stones suddenly come up with a genuine rock classic for their first self-composed single release. Keith opens the song with the famed repetitive riff, razor sharp and metronomically precise. Jones scatters lead lines all over the track while Wyman rumbles along on a heavy bassline, creating a thrilling, churning sonic soup. Jagger completely owns the lyric, with his 'Oh no' in the chorus leading perfectly into the riff again. This was where the Stones became great.

'Play with Fire' (Nanker Phelge)

No throwaway B-side here, as this flipside proves itself every bit as strong as the other, possibly even more so. An astonishingly mature piece of songwriting, the lyric (brilliantly delivered by a dark and moody Jagger) tells the story of a relationship with a society girl, whose lifestyle he despises. It simply oozes with decadent 1960s 'King's Road' opulence and needs nothing more than acoustic guitar and harpsichord to get the point across. The track is credited to the group identity of Nanker Phelge, which is an odd thing to do considering Jagger and Richards are the only Stones to appear on the recording (Jack Nitzsche plays harpsichord, and Phil Spector plays the bass using a detuned electric guitar, while Jagger and Richards provide vocals/ tambourine and acoustic guitar, respectively). The recording took place late at night, on the eve of the band leaving for an Australian tour, which may have contributed to the atmospheric nature of the track. It has been claimed that there is an unreleased full rock treatment of the song titled 'Mess with Fire', but this is unconfirmed as far as can be ascertained. It has also been asserted by Bill Wyman that there were different recordings of 'Play with Fire' and that the released version featuring only Mick and Keith may have been delivered to the record company by mistake (allegedly by Jagger's then-girlfriend Chrissie Shrimpton). If that is indeed true, which is certainly open to doubt, then it represents a rather fortunate accident.

'(I Can't Get No) Satisfaction' (Jagger, Richards)

Well, if 'The Last Time' was a classic single with a memorable riff, it was immediately trumped in all respects by this, still to this day probably the best known of all Stones songs, released in August 1965. The famous riff was written by Richards one night when he awoke with it in his head, and the distinctive buzzsaw tone comes from the fact that he had just acquired a fuzzbox effects pedal and was keen to try it out. He has said that he never intended that to be the final version, and indeed had a horn-driven sound more in mind, but once it was recorded it was clear that they had a winner. The song has everything: apart from that riff, it has a great lyric by Jagger expressing frustration, disillusionment and contempt directed at the increasingly frantic mass-media world and in particular the treadmill the Stones were on. Ironically, one of the reasons Richards didn't get his wish to try re-recording the track was precisely because their schedule of, as the song has it, 'riding round the world, doing this and signing that...' allowed for no such luxury of time. He couldn't get any satisfaction, indeed. It's no exaggeration to say that this chart-topping single changed the face of popular music at the time.

'The Spider and The Fly' (Nanker Phelge)

Another Nanker Phelge B-side, and it is becoming clear that this is a way to share some royalties with the rest of the band. This one does have a more realistic claim to be a group composition, however, being another of those loping, lazy blues songs that the early Stones were so adept at. This is an excellent example of the form, with Richards and Jones locked in tight to the rhythm while Jagger blows harmonica over the top. The song tells the on-the-road story about Jagger being in a hotel and torn between his conscience and the spider-like temptation of a lady. It's a good, humorously told tale, but it isn't exactly a 'whodunnit'!

The Rolling Stones Now! (1965) - *US Only Release*

Personnel:
Mick Jagger: vocals, harmonica
Keith Richards: guitar, vocals
Brian Jones: guitar, harmonica, vocals
Bill Wyman: bass guitar, vocals
Charlie Watts: drums and percussion
With
Ian Stewart: piano
Jack Nitzsche: piano

Record Label: London (US)
Recorded: Feb-Sept 1964, produced by Andrew Loog Oldham
US release date: October 1964
Highest chart places: US: 3
Running time: 30:50

This US-only album contained mostly previously-issued material from the UK or from US singles, but did contain two tracks unreleased at the time

Tracklisting:

'Everybody Needs Somebody to Love'
(see section *The Rolling Stones No 2*)

'Down Home Girl'
(see section *The Rolling Stones No 2*)

'You Can't Catch Me'
(see section *The Rolling Stones No 2*)

'Heart Of Stone'
(see section *Out Of Our Heads*)

'What A Shame'
(see section *The Rolling Stones No 2*)

'Mona (I Need You Baby)'
(see section *The Rolling Stones*)

'Down The Road Apiece'
(see section *The Rolling Stones No 2*)

'Off The Hook'

(see section *The Rolling Stones No 2*)

'Pain In My Heart'

(see section *The Rolling Stones No 2*)

'Oh Baby (We Got A Good Thing Goin')'

(see section *Out Of Our Heads*)

'Little Red Rooster'

(see section *The Rolling Stones*, Related Songs)

'Surprise Surprise' (Jagger, Richards)

This rather average R&B shuffle has a more interesting history than its musical content in many ways. It did not see a release in the UK at the time, and apart from this US release it only appeared in of all places the Philippines, on a various artists compilation by Decca entitled *14* – hazard a guess how many tracks were on that one? Bizarrely, in 1971, when 'Street Fighting Man' was given a three years overdue single release by Decca, this track was chosen as the B-side. Few more unlikely bedfellows can be imagined.

Out of Our Heads (1965)

Personnel:
Mick Jagger: vocals
Keith Richards: guitar, vocals
Brian Jones: guitar, harmonica
Bill Wyman: bass guitar
Charlie Watts: drums and percussion
With
Ian Stewart: piano, marimba

Record Label: Decca (UK), London (US)
Recorded: Nov 1964 – Sept 1965, produced by Andrew Loog Oldham
UK release date: September 1965. US release date: July 1965 (different tracklisting)
Highest chart places: UK: 2, US: 1
Running time: UK: 29:36 US: 33:24

The US tracklisting omitted six tracks from the UK version, with the only song included which did not get a UK release being the closing 'One More Try', which is discussed below in this section. The remainder of the US release is made up of singles, plus a live track from the UK EP *Got Live If You Want It.*

Album Facts:

Things are really getting confusing between the UK and US releases by this time. On this occasion, the album was issued with the same title in the US, but the version they put together had only six songs out of twelve in common with its UK counterpart. Once again, they filled the void with singles and B-sides, making for an arguably strong listen but going against the band's preferred policy of not including singles or B-sides on albums at this stage. To make things even odder, the US album was released in July 1965 while the band were still recording the album up until September! Looking at the official UK tracklisting, the obvious thing to notice is the very short running time of fewer than 30 minutes – indeed, side one of the original vinyl ran to a paltry 13:39, spread across six tracks! Still, albums were generally shorter in those days, and the saying has it that quality, as opposed to quantity, should rule the day. The question was, did it? Certainly, it was somewhat surprising, and perhaps disappointing, that the album still contained only four original compositions after the previous two single releases.

Historical note: only a few days before the UK release of this album, while on tour in Germany, Keith Richards met for the first time the woman who would soon become very significant in his life – Italian/German Anita Pallenberg...

Album Cover:

The cover this time out is an interesting one, featuring as it does a monochrome shot of the band looking rather claustrophobically posed in a narrow gap between what are, apparently, a pair of dumpsters. It certainly has a slightly menacing air, as if they are out and about on some nefarious business – probably involving the honour of the nation's daughters, such was the distrust of the band from the more conservative quarters at the time. The photo is by the noted photographer Gered Mankowitz, early in his career. The band name and album title appear on the cover for the first time in the UK – though the band's name is accompanied by a mysterious asterisk which has, to my knowledge, never been fully explained. The rear cover was much the same as the previous two – band photos, tracklisting and some more Loog Oldham ramblings. This time white on a black background however, which was a bit cooler, and more in touch with their image.

The US cover is all over the place. Not only is it an entirely different design, but it also features another photo from the session that produced the second album. Not to worry, however, as the 'proper' UK cover would turn up soon after on an album called *December's Children (And Everybody's)* which again was unique to the US and would feature the *Out of Our Heads* songs that were displaced on this one. Are you keeping up at the back there? Fortunately, in a couple of albums' time, this foolishness would stop once and for all, with albums being consistent across territories – with the exception of, sometimes, compilations.

'She Said 'Yeah'' (Bono, Jackson)

The 'Bono' in the songwriting credits here is in fact none other than Sonny Bono, later of 'And Cher' fame, and was originally the B-side of a Larry Williams single 'Bad Boy' in 1958. At only a minute and a half, it is hardly substantial, but it is delivered with some verve and at a frantic pace, opening the album quite effectively. The world really didn't need to hear Mick Jagger singing 'dum deedle dee dum dum' again any time soon though.

'Mercy, Mercy' (Covay, Miller)

The original version of this song was recorded by its composer, singer/songwriter Don Covay, with his band The Goodtimers, in 1964. The session was notable for one of the first appearances on record by a certain Jimi Hendrix. It's a very strong soulful pop song, with a strong chorus delivered in fine style by Jagger, while Jones plays the intro in a quite similar manner to the young Hendrix on the original – although in Jimi's playing the seeds of his famous 'Little Wing' intro can plainly be heard. Interestingly, Covay would cross paths with the Stones again some two decades later, when he provided vocals on the 1986 track 'Harlem Shuffle'.

'Hitch Hike' (Gaye, Paul, Stevenson)

It's the turn of Marvin Gaye this time, as the Stones take on this 1962 single by the soul legend. It's not really an essential work, though there is nice, albeit brief, guitar solo featured. The original Gaye version spawned one of the weakest of the endless early '60s 'dance crazes' in the form of the 'hitch hike' dance, with the thumb being alternately thrust back over the right and left shoulders. One can only hope Mr Jagger did not lower himself to that while recording this!

'That's How Strong My Love Is' (Jamison)

This borderline-schmaltzy soul ballad by Memphis songwriter Roosevelt Jamison (also recorded by Otis Redding) could easily have gone very wrong. Happily, however, this is an excellent version. Jagger's vocals display real bluesy soul, in a style very reminiscent of his contemporary, the young Van Morrison, while the band's accompaniment is rich, bold and almost lush in tone. Richards plays the only guitar on the track – Jones allegedly plays organ, but if so, it appears to be inaudible. Listen out at the 58-second mark for a rather clumsy edit in the chorus, given away by the drums. Once you've heard it, you will always notice it...

'Good Times' (Cooke)

They're really bringing in the soul big guns now, with Sam Cooke next up after Marvin and Otis. Recorded just five months after Cooke's untimely death (he was shot and killed in a Los Angeles hotel), it is certainly a lesser example of his craft, coming over as something of a retread of his 'Wonderful World' and 'Twisting the Night Away' hits. From Watts' casual drum intro onward, the Stones perform it in a laid-back, relaxed fashion which is smooth enough yet altogether devoid of excitement, and Jagger's 'Whoah la la, ta ta' delivery sounds very awkward. They had really moved beyond this sort of thing by now.

'Gotta Get Away' (Jagger, Richards)

The first original composition on the album, and it's not a bad one. Far from the bluesy R&B/soul template of many of their chosen covers, the song is more in the vein of a pop rocker such as 'The Last Time', albeit nowhere near as good. The jangling 12-string guitar provides a slight Byrds feel to proceedings, while Jagger gives a decent vocal performance, ably supported by Richards' background vocals. The (slightly superfluous) handclaps and tambourine are provided by the songwriter and producer James W. Alexander, incidentally.
In the US, the song was used as the B-side to the single 'As Tears Go By', but left off their version of the album – it turned up on the following *December's Children* release.

'Talkin' 'Bout You' (Berry)

Back to Chuck Berry for the Side Two opener, although on this occasion the deeper vaults are plundered for this relatively minor 1961 single, originally titled 'I'm Talking About You'. The song is slowed down quite noticeably from Berry's original, giving it a more insistent, serious air, and is arguably an improvement, but it is still far from a classic song and one wonders how come it came to be selected. Richards is the star here, contributing an effective solo and the main rhythm part, though Jones does back him up with some nicely placed power chords. It's efficient if unspectacular.

'Cry to Me' (Russell)

Jagger is superb on this slow, bluesy, soulful number originally recorded by Solomon Burke in 1961, wringing every ounce of emotion that he can from the lyric. Backed up by a literally weeping-sounding guitar and a beautiful, lazy bassline, this is a top-drawer rendition which easily tops Burke's version. The song was written by Bert Berns (under the name Bert Russell), a US songwriter and producer who wrote (or co-wrote) a host of familiar songs, including 'Twist and Shout', 'Hang On Sloopy', 'Here Comes the Night', 'A Little Bit of Soap' and 'Piece of My Heart'. Berns was also the 'B' in BANG Records, formed in 1965 and the early home of Neil Diamond among others, and was the regular producer for Van Morrison and Them, before he sadly died in 1967 at the age of 38, as a result of lifelong heart problems.

'Oh Baby (We Got A Good Thing Going)' (Ozen)

The 'Ozen' behind this track was an American singer, guitarist and songwriter named Barbara Lynn Ozen, who had a string of fairly minor hits in the US in the 1960s. The Stones transform the hard-driven original into a guitar-led, driving rocker which has Mick and Keith in their element, trading licks and vocal exhortations and clearly thoroughly enjoying themselves across the sadly brief two-minute duration. The track had originally been released in the US on the album *The Rolling Stones Now!* in February 1965.

'Heart of Stone' (Jagger, Richards)

The second original composition, and an excellent one at that. Deservedly well-known owing to its appearance on compilations, the song has Jagger in the role of a womaniser who meets a woman who is different, and who he adamantly vows will not break his 'heart of stone'. The verses have a slight country music influence to them (the band would flirt with Country more and more regularly in the coming years), married very effectively to the blues, and the chorus has an unstoppable feel to it, as if the singer is desperately trying to convince himself. In the US, the song had been released as a single as far back as December 1964, reaching number 19, and had subsequently appeared on the album *The Rolling Stones Now!* before getting this long overdue British release.

'The Under Assistant West Coast Promotion Man' (Nanker Phelge)

A true-life inspiration is behind this sardonic attack on the record industry, with the unfortunate subject being London Records PR man George Sherlock, who had accompanied the band on their first US tour. Musically the track is an enjoyable twelve-bar romp which might otherwise be unremarkable, but Jagger's joyously pointed delivery of the barbs in the lyric make it a stand-out in their songwriting development, while the wordy title appears to be a nod toward the types of song titles Bob Dylan had begun producing.

Note: this track marks the final recorded appearance of the Nanker Phelge credit. The song was the B-side of 'Satisfaction' in the US.

'I'm Free' (Jagger, Richards)

This folksy, jangly twelve-string-laden album closer was to become much better known in the UK 25 years later, when The Soup Dragons scored a top five hit with their version in 1990. It's an excellent song, with typically '60s lyrical content about liberation and independence, and an effortless sing-along quality. The track was chosen as the B-side to 'Get Off of My Cloud' in the US.

Related Songs:

'One More Try' (Jagger, Richards)

The only song from the US version of *Out Of Our Heads* which was unreleased in the UK, this closing track from the US version of the album is another fairly uninspired bluesy R&B shuffle from the still patchy Stones writing camp. It's less than two minutes long, and the band – Jagger in particular – seem to be rushing it, almost as if they can't wait to finish.

'Get Off of My Cloud' (Jagger, Richards)

The singles just keep getting better and better. Tired of being nagged constantly by people demanding a follow-up to 'Satisfaction', Jagger came up with the phrase 'get off of my cloud', to mean 'stop bugging me', and wrote this superb lyric about the alienation and isolation inherent in modern life, and particularly that of a rock star. The opening couplet 'I live in an apartment on the 99th floor of my block / I sit at home looking out the window imagining the world has stopped' conveys that image in such a concise and powerful way that it was rapidly becoming clear what a gifted lyricist Mick was turning into. The song is driven along by a chord sequence which, while it may not have been exactly original (see 'Louie Louie', 'Twist and Shout' and other big hits of the period), nevertheless avoids the trap of sounding derivative and gives the track an irresistible stop-start momentum which finds its release only in the angst-ridden cry of the chorus. Released in the UK in October 1965, the single was another chart-topper on both sides of the Atlantic. Incidentally, the person who is 'all dressed up just like a Union Jack' in the first verse is a reference to Screaming Lord Sutch, the horror-themed, highly theatrical singer who later led the Monster Raving Loony Party for a lengthy time in UK politics, until his suicide in 1999.

'The Singer Not the Song' (Jagger, Richards)

The B-side to 'Get Off of My Cloud' in the UK was this pleasant yet oddly Beatles-sounding jangly pop tune. It passes by in likeably unremarkable fashion until the bizarre final high note, whereupon Jagger appears to be aiming for the market where only dogs can hear him. It's an intriguing title which promises more than the song delivers, unfortunately. Quintessential flip-side fodder.

'19th Nervous Breakdown' (Jagger Richards)

And the classics keep on coming. The Stones' first release of 1966 was another densely-worded track with an often hard to decipher yet brilliant lyric concerning a spoilt society 'rich girl' of Jagger's acquaintance. It bears some similarities to 'Play with Fire' in its scathing depictions of decadent, privileged society and the hypocrisy it can conceal. The intriguing reference to the girl's father 'still perfecting ways of making sealing wax' is often taken to be a metaphorical way of saying that he is out of touch with reality and the modern world, and in particular the needs of his family. It is a lyric which reveals, in lines such as this, the increasing – and often overlooked – subtlety and sophistication present in Jagger's writing. Musically, the song powers along like a runaway train, only saved from going off the rails by the superlative rhythm section of Wyman and Watts, with Charlie's cymbal crashes constantly being used in exactly the right way to add maximum drama, and the rock-solid bass only becoming noticeable on the memorable 'dive-bombing' descending runs towards the song's end. The verses are aided breathlessly by a perfect application of the classic 12-bar chord change, and overall every trick in the book is applied to make this one of the band's most underrated singles, despite its number one status again.

'As Tears Go By' (Jagger, Richards, Oldham)

This track had already been written a couple of years previously and recorded by Marianne Faithfull, for whom it was a top ten hit in 1964. It was actually one of the first songs Mick and Keith wrote together, and the story behind its composition goes that Andrew Loog Oldham (who gets a writing credit) allegedly shut the pair in a room with orders not to come out until they had written a song utterly unlike anything they had done before, with no blues, no R&B and no sex. Both Jagger and Richards have said that at the time they thought it was sentimental rubbish, but this is a grossly unfair assessment. In fact, it is a beautiful song, with an astonishingly mature lyric about a person (supposedly intended to be a woman) looking back nostalgically and wistfully over her life. When the Stones finally recorded this, their own version, they changed the arrangement dramatically from Faithfull's take, removing all of the percussion and slowing the tempo significantly, arguably producing a far superior end result. As with 'Play with Fire', Mick and Keith are the only Stones to appear on the track, with just strings (arranged by Mike Leander) joining them on the recording. In the US it appeared on the album *December's Children*, and also as a single in its own right.

'Sad Day' (Jagger, Richards)

The B-side to the US single release of '19th Nervous Breakdown', this track never got an official UK release until it was bafflingly released as a single by Decca in 1973, and it is understandable why, to be blunt. A throwaway pop-rock song with nothing to mark it as distinctive except for some rather discordant and out-of-place sounding proto-psychedelic guitar parts coming in now and then, it simply isn't particularly good. When it was put out as a single, it flopped completely. As it would.

'Blue Turns to Grey' (Jagger, Richards)

This track which appeared on the US album *December's Children* never had an official UK release, apart from a 1971 unofficial compilation album entitled *Stone Age*, though it was picked up and covered as a successful single release by Cliff Richard and The Shadows. A somewhat reflective mid-tempo pop-ballad, the song actually has much to recommend it, both in the Stones version and also the Shadows cover, which was certainly equally worthy.

'Look What You've Done' (Waters)

This Muddy Waters cover is another track which made its only appearance on the *December's Children* album, though on this occasion it is understandable, as this is a pedestrian blues workout distinguished only by some good harmonica work from Jones. As with the above track, this one turned up in 1971 on the *Stone Age* compilation album of rarities, which was publicly disowned by the band.

December's Children (And Everybody's) – *US Only Release*

There are no recording or personnel credits applicable to this album, since it was taken entirely from other sources and previous recording sessions. Bill Wyman himself declared it to be essentially a compilation album, and gave it scant coverage in his book *Rolling With The Stones*. Even the cover was recycled from the UK *Out Of Our Heads* album.

'She Said Yeah'

(see section *Out Of Our Heads*)

'Talkin' 'Bout You'

(see section *Out Of Our Heads*)

'You Better Move On' (Alexander)

From the undistinguished early UK EP of covers entitled *The Rolling Stones*, this version of an Asher Alexander song was probably the most successful track on that EP (the others were 'Poison Ivy', 'Bye Bye Johnny' and 'Money'), showcasing a more soulful approach which stood out in their repertoire at that time, but by late 1965 it sounded unremarkable and very much 'yesterday's news'

'Look What You've Done'

(see section *Out Of Our Heads*, Related Songs)

'The Singer Not The Song'

(see section *Out Of Our Heads*, Related Songs)

'Route 66' (Troup)

Live version from the UK EP *Got Live If You Want It*

'Get Off Of My Cloud'

(see section *Out Of Our Heads*, Related Songs)

'I'm Free'

(see section *Out Of Our Heads*)

'As Tears Go By'

(see section *Out Of Our Heads*, Related Songs)

'Gotta Get Away'

(see section *Out Of Our Heads*)

'Blue Turns To Grey'

(see section *Out Of Our Heads*, Related Songs)

'I'm Moving On' (Snow)

Rocked up live version of (country singer) Hank Snow's song from the UK EP *Got Live If You Want It*. It is raw and formative, but does have an undeniable power. Like the rest of the EP, there is audience screaming throughout.

Aftermath (1966)

Personnel:
Mick Jagger: vocals, harmonica
Keith Richards: guitar, vocals, bass
Brian Jones: guitar, harmonica, various stringed instruments
Bill Wyman: bass
Charlie Watts: drums and percussion
With
Ian Stewart: piano, organ
Jack Nitzsche: piano, organ, percussion

Record Label: Decca (UK), London (US)
Recorded: Dec 1965, March 1966, produced by Andrew Loog Oldham.
UK release date: April 1966. US release date: June 1966 (different tracklisting)
Highest chart places: UK: 1, US: 2
Running time: UK: 53:20 US: 42:52

The US track listing omitted four tracks from the UK version ('Mother's Little Helper', 'Out Of Time', 'Take It Or Leave It' and 'What To Do'), with the only song added being 'Paint It Black'. Accordingly, the US version of the album is over ten minutes shorter than the, admittedly extremely long, UK version.

Album Facts:

Once again, we have a differing US edition, this time featuring the single 'Paint It Black' in place of four songs from the UK edition, as well as a different cover. However, this foolishness was slowly coming to an end, and within a year or so would finally stop. The world was getting smaller with improvements in mass media, transport and communications, and different releases for different markets started to make less and less sense. The album is full of firsts: it was the first Stones album to consist entirely of original compositions, the first to be recorded entirely in the US and their first to be released in true stereo format. It is also one of the first rock albums to be longer than 50 minutes (extraordinary for the time) and also one of the first to feature a song clocking in at over ten minutes. Fans need not have feared a mass revision of their musical style – no Frank Zappa experimental freak-outs here – but this was a massive step forward in the band's evolution.

Brian Jones leaves most of the guitar work to Richards on this one, as he experiments with more instruments, including the sitar, dulcimer, marimba and mandolin. Richards also backs Wyman's bass on three songs with fuzz bass parts, strengthening the sound. The album's release was delayed for a short while after they became embroiled in a dispute with their record companies on both sides of the Atlantic, over Oldham's initial plans to title the album 'Could You Walk on The Water', accompanied by a cover photo of the band walking over a reservoir. It didn't take a genius to figure out how that would play out at a time when the 'Bible Belt' area of the US was seeing mass burnings of Beatles albums after John Lennon's reasonably logical yet ill-advised comment that the band were more popular than Jesus in the culture of the day. Battle duly won by the record labels, the title *Aftermath* was then decided on.

Interesting fact: none of the songs on Side Two of this album have ever been performed live by the band.

Album Cover:

After his original insane plan for sacrilegious offensiveness backfired, and his 'walking on the water' concept was withdrawn (remember, two full years after this a cover was axed because it featured a toilet cubicle!), and also his plan to have a booklet of photographs accompanying the record proved impractical, Oldham nevertheless went ahead and designed the UK album cover. In place of his original grand designs, the front cover simply featured a photo of the band (taken by Guy Webster) in monochrome and heavily shadowed against an ominous dirty pink background, aligned at a 45-degree angle, with the title of the album split into two with a line bar. The band name once again did not appear. It is a simple design but nonetheless an effective one, with the band looking darker and more dangerous than ever. The back cover featured four band shots in monochrome, in the same style as the front, alongside tracklisting and credits, all in black on white. There are sleeve notes, but instead of Oldham's usual arty nonsense they were this time written by engineer Dave Hassinger and are actually directly related to the songs. Oldham was credited as 'Sandy Beach' for the design work, for no discernible reason.

The US cover again went its own way, with a colour cover photo of the band (by noted photographer David Bailey) heavily blurred in a misguided attempt to cash in on the nascent 'psychedelic' scene on an album which featured little if any such music. It is a very poor design.

'Mother's Little Helper' (Jagger, Richards)

An unusual opener to the album in terms of its sound, this cautionary tale of tired suburban housewives using pep-pills of indeterminate type to get through the day has a jaunty, almost vaudevillian sound which is rather reminiscent of Kinks' songs of the time, such as 'Dedicated Follower of Fashion'. It's an irresistibly upbeat and catchy song which goes intentionally against the grain of its rather dark message, and is in a way all the better for it. Jones plays mandolin on this one, but the key instrument producing the distinctive oriental-sounding 'twang' is an electric twelve-string guitar played with a bottleneck slide. Jack Nitzsche is credited with playing the 'Nitzsche-phone', which in reality was simply an invented credit for an ordinary piano, in order to appear mysterious. Rich acoustic guitar backing meanwhile gives the folky, tumbling feel to proceedings. The track was omitted from the US album but was released as a single there, with 'Lady Jane' on the flip.

'Stupid Girl' (Jagger, Richards)
The first really chauvinistic lyric from the band, this track is a failure not exactly because of the lyrical attitude but because of the artless and musically humdrum way it is executed. In contrast to the similarly 'misogynistic' 'Under My Thumb' from this same album, which works very successfully, 'Stupid Girl' is little more than a rant without any well-crafted musical redemption. Jagger later commented that he was influenced by some of the women he was having a bad time with during that period, while Richards claims they were influenced by the types of character they would by necessity encounter on the road. It's not a high point of the album.

'Lady Jane' (Jagger, Richards)
In complete contrast to the preceding diatribe, here we have a stately, almost Elizabethan sounding ballad – with lyrics Richards has described as being 'Chaucer English'. It has been suggested that the 'Lady Jane' in question is Jane Seymour, Lady Jane Grey or, in more contemporary fashion, Jane Ormsby-Gore, the society girl and sister of Alice Ormsby-Gore, Eric Clapton's future partner during his 'heroin years'. In actual fact, the inspiration behind the name is rather more prosaic: Jagger had recently finished reading the infamous book Lady Chatterley's Lover, in which 'Lady Jane' was used as a reference to the female genitalia, shall we say! There is no truth to rumours about it referencing marijuana. Jagger says that he intentionally used historical names, but that any connection between them referring to actual people from the same period was unconscious. Whatever the lyrical truths and origins, it is certainly a lovely song. Jagger and Richards are backed only by Jones on dulcimer and Nitzsche on harpsichord, which is an unusual instrumental line-up to say the least.

'Under My Thumb' (Jagger, Richards)
Another potentially contentious lyric here, as this song deals with Jagger turning the tables and controlling a previously very overbearing woman. Where it wins out over 'Stupid Girl', however, is firstly because it is an engaging and well-constructed song, but also because of the very fact that it was the woman who was the controlling figure originally, and it is therefore a 'poetic justice' tale in the vein of The Taming of The Shrew, rather than simple malice. Musically it is very much a 'dance' number, quite unusual for the band at this time, as evidenced by the fact that a cover by singer Wayne Gibson became a huge hit on the UK Northern Soul scene, eventually even making the Top 20 on re-release in 1974. The main hook of the track comes from Brian Jones playing the marimba – certainly unconventional as a lead instrument! Richards handles all of the guitars here, while the faithful Ian Stewart again handles thankless piano duties, not that anyone noticed.

'Doncha Bother Me' (Jagger, Richards)
This song, which sees Jagger urging an unknown acolyte to stop copying

everything he does, is certainly one of the 'second division' tracks on the album, though it is entertaining enough for what is, essentially, little more than a straight up-tempo blues number, albeit with some nice slide guitar from Jones. This time the piano is indeed audible; in fact too much so, as it is a particularly irritating honky-tonk barrelhouse variety. There are some decent lyrical ideas from Jagger, such as the line which claims 'the lines around my eyes are protected by a copyright law', but overall it is filler.

'Goin' Home' (Jagger, Richards)

If there was one real talking point which outdid all others on *Aftermath*, it would be this lengthy bluesy jam. An unremarkable song in itself, to say the least, the band simply continue jamming around the progression, stretching it out for an unheard-of eleven minutes. The instrumentation here is sparse and simple, with Jones on harmonica and Richards handling the guitar duty. Ian Stewart hammers along on piano while the other regular, Nitzsche, contributes some hand-held percussion. Once the band reach the four-and-a-half-minute mark the tempo is increasing and Jagger is leaving the lyrics behind entirely, and we're away down what in 1966 would have counted as the rabbit hole. While the piece overall does not sound too special to modern ears, its importance in breaking down song timing restrictions for 'pop' records cannot be underestimated. This is not to suggest that the track is without its musical merit today – indeed, it possesses an urgent, hypnotic quality which is still quite exciting, but its true legacy is historic.

'Flight 505' (Jagger, Richards)

The second side of the album opens with this interesting tale of Jagger boarding a plane which was destined to crash. He is sitting at home happily, when he suddenly has a realisation that he needs a different life and phones the airline to book himself on Flight 505, without having any idea where the plane is heading. As one does, of course. Happily enjoying himself once on board, it suddenly becomes apparent that there is trouble, and the pilot puts the plane down in the sea. The common misconception about this song, which has in fact been repeated so much that it has achieved 'urban myth' status, is that Flight 505 was the plane Buddy Holly crashed in, but this is incorrect. Not only was that a privately chartered plane, and would have had no such flight number, it of course crashed on dry land. Even if it had been assigned a flight number, as a Northbound flight it would, in any case, have had an even number, therefore that theory can be discredited. However, Bill Wyman has claimed, in his book Stone Alone, that 505 was actually the flight number of the plane the Stones took on their first US tour in 1964.

Musically the song is quite unusual in several ways. Firstly, it opens with a short introduction featuring a muffled-sounding tinkling piano, which ends up briefly playing the riff from 'Satisfaction' just as the drums usher the band in at much higher volume. The rhythm section largely carries this track, as the drums are extremely prominent in the mix and the bass is boosted by a fuzz bass part which, it has to be said, is occasionally a little intrusive. Interesting though, and a genuine Stones 'deep cut', which many people have never heard.

'High and Dry' (Jagger, Richards)

This 'down-home' sounding song sees an early example of the 'country Stones' in full 'sittin' on the front porch drinkin' moonshine' glory. It's not a song to take at all seriously, but it is fun in its way – if not begging for too many repeat plays. Lyrically the song begins as a standard 'girl left me' affair, with Jagger bemoaning that he has been suddenly left 'high and dry' without a warning. There is a twist, however, as we then discover that he was only after her money anyway, and he speculates that this must be the reason she left him. It's not exactly deep philosophical genius, granted, but there is at least a little sting in the tail to spice it up.

'Out of Time' (Jagger, Richards)

Here comes that marimba again! Right from the introduction of this great pop-rock track, Brian Jones is up close and personal with that tinkly marimba sound once again. The song, dealing with Jagger snubbing a girl who wants to walk back into his life after a long time away, is brilliantly written, with a soaring chorus that would deservedly reach the top of the UK charts when released by Chris Farlowe later in 1966 – although it must be said that the marimba is this time perhaps overdone and a little bit out of place.

The track was omitted from the US version of the album, but a different version (two minutes shorter than the 5:37 on the UK *Aftermath*) was released a year later on the US-only compilation album *Flowers*. A third version appeared later, in 1975, on the out-takes album Metamorphosis and as a single, featuring a Jagger demo vocal and the backing track from the Farlowe recording. In actual fact, this latter version is excellent, with an added female vocal part really lifting proceedings.

'It's Not Easy' (Jagger, Richards)

This driving rocker is another featuring the fuzz bass, which in this particular case works to the song's advantage, giving it a sort of cushion to ride on throughout its duration. Other than that, it isn't too memorable, with Jagger bemoaning being left living on his own after his girl left him, in a rather repetitive chorus to be honest. It is entertaining in its way, but a bridging track.

'I Am Waiting' (Jagger, Richards)

This lyrically oblique song is a complete change of pace, and one of the most intriguing tracks on the album, both musically and in terms of its meaning. Jagger sings vaguely about waiting for 'someone to come in from somewhere', without elaborating further, and there have been several interpretations ranging from a relationship through to the narrator's own true self emerging in a metaphysical sense when times become trying. It has also been suggested that the song is about waiting for death, a theory which is not without some merit when considering lines such as 'Well, it happens all the time, It's censored from our minds, You'll find out / Slow or fast, slow or fast, Oh yeah, oh yeah, End at last, end at last'.

This lyrical obfuscation is compounded by the unusual structure of the music, which is constructed in an almost backward way to the norm, beginning with the chorus rather than the verses, and also having a slow reflective chorus in contrast to the urgent, more strident delivery of the verses. Jones again plays the dulcimer here which, along with Nitzsche's harpsichord, helps to lend proceedings a slightly otherworldly feel. The contrast with the preceding track is astounding for the time this emerged when popular music was still regarded as being rather one-dimensional and predictable.

'Take It or Leave It' (Jagger, Richards)

A more conventional song now, yet still unusual as it is another acoustic based piece. Jagger laments a relationship he is having with a girl who treats him inconsistently, being alternately kind and thoughtless, and it is underpinned well by Richards' acoustic guitar accompaniment. Jones is again the restless musical explorer here, contributing bells and also a Japanese stringed instrument called a koto. Some rather cheesy 'la la la' refrains notwithstanding, it is an enjoyable and well-performed track. It was omitted from the US version.

'Think' (Jagger, Richards)

Unusually, in a similar way to 'As Tears Go By', this song had already been covered by another artist prior to its release by the Stones, with Chris Farlowe taking his version to the lower reaches of the UK charts three months earlier in January 1966. Lyrically it seems a little contradictory, with Jagger advising a girl to think back over what she has done, asking 'whose fault was that?' – however the issue he's addressing is never made clear, with the girl in question at one point appearing to be accused of not changing, yet at another being described as having grown 'old before her time'. Certainly, he seems unhappy about when they were together 'a year ago', that they were 'conning people for a dime', but beyond this we are in the dark. Sometimes a little ambiguity can be a very good thing, as with 'I Am Waiting', but in this case it does seem irritatingly contradictory of itself. Nice hook though, with some effective acoustic guitar from Jones backing up Richards' lead.

'What to Do' (Jagger, Richards)

An odd ending to the album, with this simple little pop song with Jagger bemoaning, quite simply, that there is 'nothing to do'. It's a song about being bored. And that's it. It's mid-paced with little intriguing going on musically beyond some backing vocals from Keith. It's two and a half minutes of filler to close the album, which seems somewhat anti-climactic. They left this off the US version. Perhaps wisely.

Related Songs:

'Paint It Black' (Jagger, Richards)

Included on the US version of *Aftermath* but not the UK edition, 'Paint It Black' was released in May 1966 and soon hit the Number One spot in both Britain and America. Displaying a greater mastery of light and shade than almost anything recorded by the band up to this point, the track remains an acknowledged classic and a landmark in 1960s recordings. There were claims that Brian Jones' use of the sitar on this track was merely copying George Harrison on the Beatles' 'Norwegian Wood' but, given the amount of esoteric instrumentation Jones utilised on the *Aftermath* album, this seems a rather harsh assessment. The original idea for the song came out of Bill Wyman playing around on the organ, of all unlikely scenarios, but Keith Richards' later claim that the song began as a spoof, with Wyman imitating the playing of original manager Eric Eastman and Watts supplying a deliberately stiff 'B-movie soundtrack' drum pattern, is open to conjecture. What is certain is that a magnificent record arose from this beginning. Jagger's vocal alternates to great effect between dark introspection and howling rage, and midway through the track Watts contributes one of the great drum breaks of the decade after the line 'I could not foresee this thing happening to you'. It really conjures up the howling grief of someone who has lost a close friend or relative and is surely far from what anyone would have expected from the band. It has been claimed that the inspiration for the lyric came from Jagger reading James Joyce's impenetrable book Ulysses, which contains the line 'I have to turn my head until my darkness goes', but again this is unproven. Interestingly, the first release of the single added a comma, making the title 'Paint It, Black', but this was subsequently removed for all future releases.

'Long Long While' (Jagger, Richards)

The Stones' soul influences come to the fore again here with this somewhat overwrought ballad, which is certainly a good listen, but sounds a little as if they wrote and recorded it in thirty minutes - which, given their output and songwriting craft at the time, may not be too far from the truth. It gained later popularity after its use in a key scene in the 1995 Robert De Niro film Casino, directed by Martin Scorsese (himself a long-time Stones admirer who went on to direct the band's 2008 concert film Shine A Light).

'Have You Seen Your Mother, Baby, Standing in The Shadow?' (Jagger, Richards)

Lyrically baffling and musically unexpected, this was yet another curveball thrown by the Stones, whose constant invention and capacity to surprise at this time is severely underestimated. It's anyone's guess what Jagger was alluding to in the lyric – suggestions through the years have included prostitution, corrupt politicians and even a choice between birth and abortion – but like many Stones songs, whatever the meaning it is certainly a lot darker in its theme than it sounds on a cursory listen. Musically it is unusual for the band as it is driven by a horn section (again arranged by Mike Leander, who arranged 'As Tears Go By'), the first of their tracks to feature this accompaniment. Keith Richards has gone on record as saying that he hated the mix, as the rhythm section lost all of its power, but opinion is divided among fans. Its chart placings of 5 and 9 in the UK and US respectively were something of a disappointment after the last few singles.

The American sleeve featured a photo of the band in bizarre drag outfits as old women (there was also a video featuring the same theme), and they all adopted names for their new personas: 'Penelope' Wyman (in wheelchair), 'Flossie' Jones, 'Molly' Richard, 'Sarah' Jagger and the hideous apparition that is Watts' alter-ego Millicent. After the photo shoot they kept their outfits on, went straight round to a bar and had a drink while watching TV, as if nothing was untoward! They performed the track on The Ed Sullivan Show soon afterwards but had to mime as Jones had his arm in a cast – supposedly an injury sustained punching a wall. Nitzsche plays piano on the track, and the studio logs also credit Jones as doing the same.

'Who's Driving Your Plane?' (Jagger, Richards)

Another 12-bar blues for the flipside, with definite echoes of Dylan this time (there is a noticeable resemblance to 'Leopard Skin Pill-Box Hat'), heavy and powerful enough but unremarkable. Jagger bemoans a girl who is so easily led that she appears to have no will of her own, in a lyric which is surely the only time 'Tiffany Lamps' have been mentioned in a rock song.

'Ride On, Baby' (Jagger, Richards)

Recorded during the *Aftermath* sessions, but only released two years later on the US compilation *Flowers*. A strong pop-rock song, it would have made a good inclusion on *Aftermath*, as it is stronger than some of the tracks which actually made the cut. Featuring Jones on harpsichord and marimba, as well as Richards on autoharp, the song is another biting lyrical piece, with Jagger delivering some scathing comments towards a woman of unknown origin. It includes lines such as 'You may look pretty but I can't say the same for your mind', 'Well I've seen your face in a trashy magazine / You know where you're going but I don't like the places you've been' and 'By the time you're thirty you're gonna look sixty-five / You won't look pretty and your friends will have kissed you goodbye'. Ouch! If you haven't heard this one, track it down. A real buried treasure.

'Sittin' On A Fence' (Jagger, Richards)
Another track recorded during the sessions for *Aftermath* but left on the shelf, this pleasant acoustic folk-pop song was also released as a single by a male vocal duo named Twice As Much in May 1965, six months before the band recorded it themselves. This version is arguably better than the Stones' recording, being slowed down a little and accentuating the melody better. Then again, it was recorded using the session guitar talents of a certain Jimmy Page! This time out the song was saved from Stones obscurity when their version appeared on the 1968 compilation *Through the Past Darkly*, where it was quite likely to have been used as 'bait' for fans who had all of the hits.

Between the Buttons (1967)

Personnel:
Mick Jagger: vocals, harmonica, percussion
Keith Richards: guitar, vocals, bass, piano
Brian Jones: guitar, organ, recorder, various instruments
Bill Wyman: bass
Charlie Watts: drums and percussion
With
Ian Stewart: piano, organ
Jack Nitzsche: piano, harpsichord
Nicky Hopkins: piano
Nick De Caro: accordion

Record Label: Decca (UK), London (US)
Recorded: Aug-Dec 1966, produced by Andrew Loog Oldham.
UK release date: January 1967. US release date: February 1967 (different tracklisting)
Highest chart places: UK: 3, US: 2
Running time: 38:51

Album Facts:

Once again there is a different tracklisting for the US version of the album – but thankfully this would be the last time (cue for a song...). Only two tracks are different this time out, with both sides of the single 'Let's Spend the Night Together' / 'Ruby Tuesday' displacing two tracks from the UK release.

As with the previous albums, recording was undertaken over a period of some months in between touring and other commitments. At that time the relative luxury of spending a month or so in the studio focused on the recording of an album was not an option – unless, of course, you were the Beatles and had abandoned touring by that time – and the Stones were still well and truly stuck on that treadmill in 1966. The album is the last one produced by Andrew Loog Oldham, before the band publicly fell out with him later in the year.

When the album appeared, 1967 had just dawned, with the Summer of Love mere months away. As a result, there is a difference in the album's sound, though not by any means a leap into the psychedelic zeitgeist. That would come soon enough, however.

Incidentally, the somewhat odd phrase 'between the buttons' refers to being 'undecided'. According to Watts, when he was planning the cartoons on the back cover, he asked Oldham what the album title would be. Oldham said the title was 'between the buttons', meaning it had not yet been decided. He took it literally, ran with the phrase for his poem, and it stuck.

Album Cover:

The cover photo was taken by Gered Mankowitz, in Primrose Hill, North London, after an all-night recording session at Olympic Studios in November 1966. It is claimed that the shoot took place at 5:30am, but the apparent lightness of the surroundings suggests it may have been slightly later (sunrise in London even at the beginning of November is closer to 7am). A home-made filter was used to give the blurry image of the band appearing to melt into their surroundings, intended – according to Mankowitz – to convey the image of the band being, well, stoned, after being up all night. Only Jones refused to look serious for the photo, grinning and hiding inside his collar, an attitude which frustrated the photographer at the time but which he came to see as part of the band's general 'couldn't care less' image. The band name and album title can be seen in very small font within Charlie's coat buttons.

The rear cover was dominated by a six-panel cartoon and accompanying rhythmic poem, written and drawn by Watts, indicating variable public reaction to the band and utilising the title phrase repeatedly. Note that this was the first instance in which the UK and US versions of the album used the same cover design.

'Yesterday's Papers' (Jagger, Richards)

The tone for the album is set early on with this slightly dreamy-sounding song about resolving not to be tied down again after getting out of a troubled relationship. Supposedly this was the first song written by Jagger alone but, like Lennon & McCartney's compositions, it was still credited to the partnership, and it is claimed to be written about his break-up with Chrissie Shrimpton, who was his long-term companion before Marianne Faithfull. The song's almost otherworldly feel is largely achieved by Jones' vibraphone playing being prominent throughout, with Nitzsche's harpsichord also contributing. This was some way from the blues. Incidentally, this was another Stones song which was recorded by Chris Farlowe – the fifth one from their catalogue which he had covered.

'My Obsession' (Jagger, Richards)

There is no other way to say it: this is a very odd track! Lyrically it appears to concern Jagger's obsession with a woman who he wants to control, but musically things are all over the place. There is a rumbling bassline and skittering drums giving an almost jazzy feel to this, while Stewarts's tinkling piano solo is 'out there' to the extreme. It appears to be constructed to conjure up the image of Jagger's character, with his slightly creepy obsession, and as such it has to be said that it succeeds. Does it make for three minutes of enjoyable listening? Well, the jury still requires some convincing on that one...

'Back Street Girl' (Jagger, Richards)

In his frequent dismissal of this album, Jagger has gone on record as stating that this track is the only one he actually liked. It seems odd that he would say that about the song in a way, as lyrically it is rather morally distasteful to say the least, concerning a common girl who he has as his mistress, and urges her not to try to become part of his life lest she embarrasses him. Even for a man becoming known for lyrics such as 'Stupid Girl', 'Under My Thumb' and 'Who's Driving Your Plane' this was questionable stuff. Musically it is another significant departure from the existing Stones template, being in waltz time and driven along by a French accordion played by American session musician Nick De Caro. Jones is again on the vibraphone on this one, while Watts dispenses with his drumkit altogether, utilising only tambourine and a wooden percussion instrument called claves.

The track was omitted from the US version of the album. While this may conceivably have been on moral grounds by the record label, it did not prevent it appearing on the compilation album *Flowers* not too long afterwards.

'Connection' (Jagger, Richards)

Much more of a recognisable Stones imprint here on this jerky rocking track. Written mainly by Richards, it addresses such themes as the frustration of the long hours the band had to spend in airports and things such as customs hassles. There is a LOT of rhyming with the word 'connection' here! Jones plays organ on this one, while the ever-reliable Nitzsche supplies the piano and Jagger accompanies Watts on percussion by beating a bass drum with his hands – which seems an oddly superfluous thing to do, but as long as he enjoyed himself...

Even quite recently Keith has spoken about this being his favourite overlooked Stones track (notably in a 2018 US talk show appearance), which would fit with the fact that he was apparently the key composer.

'She Smiled Sweetly' (Jagger, Richards)

The organ is the main propelling force behind this rather affecting gentle ballad, far removed from the 'Back Street Girl' lyrical thrust – notably played by Richards, as he remembers it. Oldham has commented on this, comparing it to 'Lady Jane' and 'When Tears Go By' and claiming he prefers it to those two earlier songs. He also says of Jagger's vocal that he is 'an actor, he can't sing, he acts the words', which seems a slightly harsh assessment, but you can see what he means in a sense. He has always been a man who can adopt a different persona for the track in question and get inside the song that way. According to Richards, Jones and Wyman were absent from the session, with he himself playing organ and bass; this makes the track significant as the first Stones recording to feature no guitar. Overall, one of the better tracks on the album.

'Cool, Calm & Collected' (Jagger, Richards)

A slightly avant-garde vaudevillian flavour pervades this song, which in some ways presages 'On with the Show' from the next album. It features multiple instruments by the increasingly experimental Jones, including dulcimer and a truly bizarre kazoo solo! The influence of the more English music-hall moments by the Kinks is writ large here, from the music through to Jagger's vocal, as he sings in an ever-so-refined accent about an upper-class woman who is always seemingly in control, and even when she is not, she buries her cares and maintains the impression. It has also been theorised that the lyric could be obliquely referring to Great Britain itself, characterised as a woman dressed in red, white and blue, but given Jagger's predilection for exposing the hypocrisy of the gentry in such songs as 'Play With Fire' and '19th Nervous Breakdown', that seems a trifle far-fetched. One has to say that, between his pot shots at the upper classes and his put-down of the unfortunate 'back street girl', it would appear that Jagger doesn't seem to like anyone very much! Note that there is a connection with the Kinks, as far as the sonic similarity mentioned above, as Nicky Hopkins, who plays piano on this track (beginning a long association with the band) also played on the Kinks' 'Sunny Afternoon'.

'All Sold Out' (Jagger, Richards)

Opening Side Two of the album comes 'Angry Jagger', expressing his bitterness at a girl who has betrayed him in some unidentified, but clearly malicious, way. One thing which becomes clear by this time is the number of different ways he is able to look at relationships, with he himself being either the abuser or the abused by regular turns. This should, in a way, prevent those who take offence at the crude sentiments of songs like 'Back Street Girl' or 'Under My Thumb' from doing so quite so readily, as it seems clear that he is creating a fictional dynamic for each song. What is possibly revealing at this particular point in time is that there almost always seems to be an abuser and a victim one way or another, and whether he personally plays the crass or the mistreated part, things very seldom appear to be happy.

Musically, this is very much Keith's party, with his stinging lead lines peppering the whole track and giving it an urgency and energy that much of this album lacks. Jones, on the other hand, having apparently taken a great dislike to the guitar by this point, contributes a recorder part, which doesn't really affect things in any significant way, to be honest.

'Please Go Home' (Jagger, Richards)

Psychedelic Bo Diddley. It's probably not something the world was crying out for, but it's what it got with this track. Lyrically, Jagger is again having a hard time as he begs the unidentified subject of the song to go home and get out of his life, referring to her 'devious ways'. The important thing here, however, is the overall sound, as the voice is almost treated just like another instrument to reinforce the furiously repetitive beat. As Watts in particular hammers away with metronomic precision at the familiar Diddley rhythm, all manner of studio effects are utilised to subvert the beat and subject it to a psychedelic maelstrom. Echo is applied liberally, as guitars and cymbals crash ominously, and Jones plays a modulated frequency generator called an oscillator. It's not exactly an easy sound, nor if we are honest a particularly enjoyable one, but it sure is innovative. Thankfully not any more than three and a quarter minutes of innovation, though, otherwise the title might be directed at the band from a million headache-suffering listeners... although not in the US, where the track was omitted from the album (again, it appeared later on *Flowers*).

'Who's Been Sleeping Here?' (Jagger, Richards)

The Stones do Dylan. Just as John Lennon had displayed his Dylan adulation with 'You've Got to Hide Your Love Away', so here do the Stones – although rather than the folkie Dylan to whom Lennon owed his debt, the influence here is the surreal wordplay and (to coin Dylan himself) the 'thin wild mercury sound' of his *Highway 61 Revisited / Blonde On Blonde* phase. And they do it superbly. Dylan's backing sound is evoked precisely by Watts' drumming, Jones' harmonica and Richards' lead guitar lines, sounding as if they had been scattered by Dylan's sidekick Mike Bloomfield himself. Jagger apes Dylan's trademark inflexions in his vocal, particularly in his technique of letting notes go on after the end of a line, while lyrically it is spot on. A simple plot consisting of arriving home to find someone has been sleeping there (with his girl even compared to Goldilocks to reinforce the Three Bears theme) is embellished by appeals to a cast of truly Dylan-esque characters to investigate this case. The butcher, the baker, the old cavalier, the sergeants, the soldiers, the cruel old grenadier and, lastly, even the three musketeers are all invoked before the line 'the noseless old newsboy, the old British brigadier' really plants us firmly into 'Like A Rolling Stone' territory. It's not original, though it's conversely not at all what you'd expect, but it is damned good. A pastiche or homage, but an expert one whichever view you subscribe to.

'Complicated' (Jagger, Richards)

As we have seen, much of the time Jagger plays out a role in his lyrics about a woman, but in this case, there is no doubt as to the subject: it is addressed to Marianne Faithfull, who was by now his companion. The lyric addresses the contradictions inherent in her character, though he views them as a positive thing rather than a destructive feature – a clear sign as to his feelings toward her. The song follows the 'complicated' theme musically, having a somewhat over-fussy arrangement and a slightly unfocused structure, but it survives by dint of its enthusiasm. The bass is doubled up on this track, with Wyman's familiar Vox bass joined by Richards (who also plays lead and rhythm guitar parts) on his own Fender Precision. Jones also plays some rhythm guitar, as well as organ, with Nitzsche again tinkling the piano ivories.

'Miss Amanda Jones' (Jagger, Richards)

In which the spirit of Chuck Berry is dragged out for one more turn across the Stones stage! The Berry influence is clear from the moment Keith sparks up the intro (which bears some resemblance to the later T Rex song 'Get It On'), although it is leavened by the slightly more 'pop' feel of a vocally double-tracked mid-section. It's a powerful rocker at a time when the album probably needed one, but the most interest the song has produced over the years is speculation about the title character, who is identified in the song as a 'delightfully stoned ... darling of the discotheque crowd', and seemingly also a debutante who is, however, 'losing her nobility'. Theories have included it being merely a randomly named composite of many such girls the Stones encountered or even Keith's girlfriend Anita Pallenberg, but the most common consensus is that it is most likely referring to Amanda Lear, the future muse of Salvador Dali who was seeing a lot of Brian Jones at the time.

'Something Happened to Me Yesterday' (Jagger, Richards)

A real oddity to close the album on, as Jagger recounts what is clearly an LSD trip to the backing of more vaudevillian accompaniment. In a notable first, Keith Richards gets a lead vocal spot, as he sings the choruses (in the third person) to Jagger's verses. Jones plays saxophone throughout, but there is some disagreement about his other contributions here. There is some whistling which has been identified as him, but there are also bizarre interjections from a tuba of all things – sounding not unlike the TV theme tune to Hancock's Half Hour it must be said – and some claim this is also provided by Jones. Who played what is not definitively clear, however, and the Mike Leander Orchestra take care of violins and at least some of the brass on the track, plus it surely cannot be that even the freakishly versatile Jones can play every instrument he picks up! It is a notable fact about this album that, while Jones is contributing an ever-greater variety of instruments, his core role in the band already seems to be waning significantly. This would become even more of a theme over the next couple of albums, sadly.

At the end of the song, Jagger delivers a plummy, BBC pastiche spoken word section saying goodnight from 'the boys in the band' and ending with 'So if you're out tonight, don't forget, if you're on your bike, wear white. Evening all', in clear homage to TV series Dixon of Dock Green. Once again, this track very much foreshadows the track 'On with the Show' on the next album, indicating that, far from being the isolated, slavish *Sgt Pepper* copy many have claimed, the seeds of the full-blown psychedelia of *Their Satanic Majesties Request* were planted here.

Related Songs:

'Let's Spend the Night Together' (Jagger, Richards)

The Stones court controversy yet again, with this single recorded at the same sessions as the album yet only included on the US version. It's hard to imagine now, but even in 1967, during what we like to think of as the 'Swinging Sixties', the establishment on both sides of the Atlantic reacted with blood vessel-bursting apoplexy to the suggestion of unsanctioned nocturnal activities. Jagger went on record as claiming that he meant it in terms of spending the evening together and that those making anything more of it simply had over-imaginative minds, but obviously nobody believed him. Not even himself if we're being honest.

In America, an appearance on The Ed Sullivan Show was only allowed on the ridiculous proviso that Jagger sing 'Let's spend some time together' instead. Disappointingly, unlike Jim Morrison's flouting of a similar request to remove the word 'higher' from 'Light My Fire', Jagger complied with this absurd demand, though the expression on his face when viewing footage of the show makes his feelings abundantly clear. There is a common story that, when the band reappeared back on stage after the song, they had all changed clothes into Nazi uniforms complete with swastikas, causing Sullivan to order them offstage to change again, whereupon they left the studio entirely. Sadly all research indicates that this is an urban legend, possibly growing from an infamous photo shoot that Jones did in full Nazi regalia. A pity, as it is a great story! A week after the Sullivan performance, the band incurred the wrath of the – possibly even more uptight – BBC, when they appeared on the prestigious Sunday Night at The London Palladium TV show. At the end of the show, the ludicrous conclusion was always for all of the acts to stand on a big rotating platform waving inanely at the audience. The Stones quite reasonably told them what to do with their platform and refused to stand on it, and from the BBC hierarchy's reaction (and the public, it must be said) one would think they had attacked a piñata shaped like the Queen with machetes.

Another amusing story about this track is that, according to engineer Glyn Johns, while they were recording it, two policemen appeared at the studio, after allegedly having a tip-off that something illegal was occurring. The significant amount of dope on the premises was hastily carried out of the back door while the attention of the two – supposedly starstruck – policemen was distracted by having their truncheons used as makeshift percussion instruments, banged together like claves. A tapping sound during the bridge of the song is a direct result...

In all of this – important as it underlines the image the band were successfully cultivating at this time – it should not be forgotten that 'Let's Spend the Night Together' is an extremely good song. Driven along by Nitzsche's piano (the instrument Richards composed the song on), it has an unstoppable momentum and a chorus which lodges in the brain. It failed to top the charts, reaching Number 3 in the UK and failing to crack the Top 50 entirely in the US, which was probably largely due to radio bans, especially in America.

'Ruby Tuesday' (Jagger, Richards)

On the flipside of the single (actually a double A-side) was this beautiful song, which was allegedly written as a paean to an infamous groupie – although

Keith Richards, who wrote the lyrics, claimed in his autobiography that it was written about his former girlfriend Linda Keith. She had taken up with Jimi Hendrix, getting involved in drugs and some unsavoury individuals, causing Richards to speak to her parents, warning them that he was concerned about the 'dark path' she was on (when Keith Richards says that about somebody, you listen!). Another of the Stones 'baroque' pieces, like 'Lady Jane' and 'When Tears Go By', it was listed separately on the US chart with 'Let's Spend the Night Together'. The song reached Number 1 in the Billboard chart, which seems rather odd as 'Let's Spend the Night Together' only officially reached 55, and customers were buying both sides of the record. Jones plays recorder and piano on this but, more unusually, Richards and Wyman actually played the double bass together, in the manner of a cello, with Wyman fingering the notes as Richards drew the bow across the strings!

The song was covered famously by American singer/songwriter Melanie, whose version reached the UK top 10 when it was released as a single in December 1970. Although the song is credited to Jagger/Richards, Mick has admitted he had no part in the writing, and it is generally accepted that the uncredited Brian Jones contributed to finishing the song off.

'We Love You' (Jagger, Richards)

Now this one certainly comes with some 'baggage'! Already having planned a single to be released in advance of their next album, to tie in with the 'Summer of Love', this track was actually rushed out after the events following the band's infamous drug bust earlier that year. Clearly a trumped-up charge, of which reams have been already written, suffice to say that prison sentences of twelve months and three months had been harshly handed to Keith and Mick respectively – so harshly that Times editor William Rees-Mogg was moved to write a famous editorial in support of their cause, entitled 'Who Breaks a Butterfly on a Wheel?'. This was an astonishing and courageous move on his part considering the band's anti-establishment stance. After the sentences were quashed on appeal at the end of July, the band rushed into the studio to record 'We Love You' within a few days.

A tremendous piece of peak-period psychedelia, the record bears all the hallmarks of the genre: droning, Moroccan-sounding tempo, repetitive trance-like rhythm, Mellotron, heavily treated vocals, etc. Opening with the sound of footsteps on a stone floor and a cell door slamming shut, the meaning is made immediately clear – a thank you to the fans and everyone else who had supported them (the Who, who had recorded 'The Last Time' and 'Under My Thumb' as a single in support, the Beatles, and a great many others), while also a defiant anti-establishment message. Jones plays Mellotron on the track, while Nicky Hopkins supplies the ominously repetitive piano part which he had apparently already come up with himself, and really should have earned him a writing credit. Lennon and McCartney are on backing vocals while Allen Ginsberg, who was also visiting the studio, conducted the voices from behind the glass. At the very end of the track a distorted snippet of the B-side 'Dandelion' is faded in as the coda, but on recent compilations an alternate edit has been used which omits this and instead concludes with John Lennon's voice announcing, 'Your health!'

A promotional video was produced, directed by counterculture film-maker Peter Whitehead, which included segments parodying the trial of Oscar Wilde, with Jagger cast as Wilde, Marianne Faithfull as Wilde's lover Bosie and Richards in a paper wig as the trial judge, the Marquess Of Queensberry. The drug bust which took place at Richards' home, Redlands, is also hilariously referenced in the video – during the raid, a naked Marianne Faithfull was famously reported to have been lying (and also apparently 'cavorting') scarcely covered by a sheepskin rug, and in the video such a rug is introduced as evidence, thrown onto the judge's bench! When he apparently waves away Faithfull's protestations, Jagger appears lying on the bench from under the rug, himself naked! Overall it is a record and a film which are sadly overlooked when people reminisce in misty-eyed fashion about that year, and it is a shame that the single rose no higher than Number Eight in the UK chart.

Sadly, the rapid decline of Brian Jones starts in earnest here as, having recently suffered a nervous breakdown, his appearances in the video show him in a distressingly poor state.

'Dandelion' (Jagger, Richards)

The B-side to the single is actually a far more 'immediate' song than the dense, multi-layered 'We Love You'. Another pure piece of psychedelic pop-rock, it is a tremendous song in its own right, featuring a superb vocal performance from Jagger, particularly on the uplifting chorus. Drawing its inspiration lyrically from nursery rhymes, it is nevertheless reasonable to suppose that a different form of weed may have been on the minds of its composers when they wrote it! Nicky Hopkins plays harpsichord on the track, while Jones handles Mellotron again. It has always been strongly rumoured that Lennon and McCartney again appear on backing vocals – it does sound like them – but this has never been verified. The original single version of this song has a short piano snippet of 'We Love You' faded in as a coda at the end, but this is edited off the versions on most compilation albums. The original demo of the song from December 1966, with different lyrics, originally entitled 'Sometimes Happy, Sometimes Blue'.

Their Satanic Majesties Request (1967)

Personnel:
Mick Jagger: vocals, percussion
Keith Richards: guitar, vocals
Brian Jones: Mellotron, flute, various instruments
Bill Wyman: bass, vocals, Mellotron, oscillator
Charlie Watts: drums and percussion
With
Nicky Hopkins: piano, organ, harpsichord

Record Label: Decca (UK), London (US)
Recorded: Feb-Oct 1967, produced by The Rolling Stones.
Release Date: December 1967.
Highest chart places: UK: 3, US: 2
Running time: 44:06

Album Facts:

The recording process of this most controversial of all Stones albums begin soon after the release of *Between the Buttons* and dragged on chaotically over around eight sporadic months until November 1967. Bill Wyman has claimed, in his 2002 book *Rolling with The Stones*, that a large part of the problem was due to Jagger, Richards and Jones regularly turning up with a retinue of hangers-on, most of whom would hinder the sessions rather than add anything creative. As he explains, he became extremely frustrated at this, as did Andrew Loog Oldham, who walked out of the sessions, and the Stones' career, during the recording. As a result, this album is produced by the band themselves, an arrangement which Jagger later acknowledged was not for the best.

The initial reaction to the album largely denounced it as a mere poor facsimile of *Sgt Pepper*, but this is unduly harsh on the record and time has been kind to its reputation. It has always remained the most contentious album in the band's catalogue, having admirers and decriers in equal measure – although there are a healthy number of people, particularly in later years, who enjoy parts of it without claiming it to be a work of great significance.

It was during the recording of this album that the downward spiral of Brian Jones began to develop significantly. Early in the year, while on a trip over to Morocco with Anita Pallenberg (then with Jones) and Keith Richards, Jones was rushed to hospital in France where he was admitted with pneumonia. While he recovered, Keith and Anita continued on their way and, in the absence of Jones, a relationship began to form between them, leading to the breakup of Anita and Brian after he arrived upon release from hospital. Jones took this incredibly badly, feeling humiliated and generally over-reacting in a disproportionate way, which led to him suffering a nervous breakdown. Later in the year Jones and the formidably named modern artist Prince Balthazar Klossowski de Rola (known as 'Balthus' or 'Stash') were themselves arrested for possession of cocaine and hash. Jones' subsequent prison sentence was, like those of Jagger and Richards, later quashed, but not before multiple psychiatrists testified as to his state of mind and 'irrational fears'. The slippery slope had begun.

Album Cover:

Well, where do we start with this one? The original cover came with a lenticular 3D photo of the band sitting in general fantastical costumery with Jagger in the centre in wizard's robes and a big pointy hat. That's not necessarily to say they looked ridiculous, I may add. Although to be fair they DID look ridiculous! The lenticular cover made them turn to look in different directions if viewed from different angles, though sadly this was replaced by a standard photograph for later pressings, owing to the high cost of production. In an obvious reference to the *Sgt Pepper* front cover, there was a sort of collage look to the photo, with a castle in the background, planets hanging in the sky and colourful plants and foliage at the front. As a nod to the doll with the 'Welcome the Rolling Stones' sweater on *Pepper*, the four Beatles are represented on the Stones sleeve, with their photos hidden among the flowers. It's colourful and joyous, which is marvellous in its way, but unfortunately, there is something of an air of schoolchildren making things out of cardboard and coloured paper about the whole thing. Charming amateurishness you might say. The rear cover had the track details as if embroidered onto a sort of carpet against a wildly colourful background representing the four elements, and there was even (as with *Pepper*) a gatefold sleeve this time out. The inner gatefold was an unashamed collage, consisting of all manner of things from an observatory telescope, through astronomical images and Indian mandalas to scenes from Renaissance paintings. Most bizarre of all, much of the left-hand pane was filled by a large maze, in the shape of a sort of square castle with a round tower at each corner. For some inexplicable reason, there is a large wall, or barrier, across the southern portion which makes the maze impossible to traverse, despite the welcoming pop-art lettering in the middle proclaiming 'It's Here!'

The photo on the front and the inner collage design were by Michael Cooper, while the back cover painting was by Tony Meeuwissen. Originally the whole of the front cover was supposed to be occupied by the 3D photo, but this was simply too prohibitively expensive, so it was reduced in size and a swirly 'clouds on blue sky' design used as a border. The title of the album, incidentally, was originally intended to be the dreadful 'Cosmic Christmas', until Jagger got a new inspiration after reading some of the wording in his passport. He proposed 'Her Satanic Majesty Requests and Requires', but the powers that be understandably baulked at the idea of the Queen being referred to as 'Her Satanic Majesty', so it was amended to the final title.

If all of this sounds like a huge conceit, and a mish-mash of impractical ideas, spare a thought for the poor record company executives when they were presented with the original proposed design for the cover – a photograph of Mick Jagger naked, on a cross. Yes, exactly. If the reservoir and the 'Walking on Water' title had provoked outrage, that one was never really going to get through, was it?

'Sing This All Together' (Jagger, Richards)

The opening track on the album leaves the listener in no doubt as to the territory the band has led us into. This is fairly standard hippy-dippy philosophising ('Why don't we sing this song all together / Open our heads let the pictures come'), only it is musically married to the Stones' own vision of psychedelia: that is to say dark, distorted, creepy and inhabiting a whole world apart from Pepperland. The track begins with a weird, compressed piano from Nicky Hopkins which is joined by the crazed Jones blasting out horn shrieks on his now ever-present Mellotron. The vocal part comes in with a chorus of voices dominated by Jagger, with Mick alone in the verses. There is much stereo trickery, and it is generally agreeable once you adjust your brain to accept it. A lengthy mid-section consists almost entirely of a host of weird and wonderful percussion instruments, played by a selection of unidentified (but probably also fairly weird and wonderful) people, all with Watts keeping time on his bass drum. Jones takes leave of his Mellotron long enough to play some actual real Saxophone before the song itself comes back in, by this time propelled along quite well by Jones and his horn outbursts. This was only FOUR years since 'Come On', for God's sake. We certainly weren't in Kansas anymore now, let alone Dartford...

'Citadel' (Jagger, Richards)

Segueing straight from the previous track (the album does this throughout) comes one of the standouts on the record. A great reverb-drenched guitar riff played by Keith opens proceedings (bearing more than a casual resemblance to Roxy Music's 1973 track 'Street Life') before Jagger enters with a strong vocal performance, delivering an excellent lyric which is open to all manner of interpretation. Is the titular Citadel an abstract idea relating to society, or do the references to 'concrete hills', 'dollar bills' and the chorus references to Candy and Taffy place it as being New York?

Note: one of Andy Warhol's companions in his 'Factory' was Candy Darling, whom Jagger had met by this time, and she supposedly had a friend named Taffy. Whatever the truth, it is a thought-provoking and evocative lyric which illustrates further Jagger's underrated talent as a lyricist of some note. The real hook of the song is that riff from Keith, which is a recurring theme in the track, and there is a fuzz bass mirroring the regular bassline which arrives midway through, giving the song a subtle extra burst of urgency. All in all, one of the Stones' most underappreciated masterpieces.

'In Another Land' (Wyman)

'In Another Land' is noteworthy as being written by Bill Wyman, and therefore the first song to break the Jagger / Richards songwriting stranglehold. Things might have been very different, however, as it very nearly didn't get recorded at all. Wyman had written the song on a Thomas organ at the beginning of July and made a rough demo in some studio downtime. One day in mid-July was one of the frustrating days when nobody else had turned up apart from – according to Wyman – Charlie Watts and Nicky Hopkins. They were going to give up for the day when engineer Glyn Johns asked Wyman if he had anything they could work on. He played them 'In Another Land' on the piano, and they liked it, immediately starting work on it. Wyman sings and plays bass, piano and organ, while Hopkins contributes harpsichord. Richards plays acoustic guitar on the final recording, and the cello sound is assumed to be Jones on the Mellotron, but Jagger only contributes backing vocals to the track. The Small Faces were recording next door, and Steve Marriott came in to record a vocal part for the track. Wyman was very unsure about his own lead vocal and requested that significant tremolo be added to his voice to mask any inadequacies. As a result, the otherworldly effect gives the song a totally psychedelic, dreamy quality which would not have been out of place, musically or lyrically, on Pink Floyd's debut album.

The track was deemed to be strong enough to release as a single in the US in December 1967, but the circumstances of its release were inexplicable to say the least. Instead of putting it out as a Stones single, they instead released it credited to 'Bill Wyman', even though the B-side was the fellow album track 'The Lantern'. Add to that the minimal publicity put behind the single, and the record company would appear to have deliberately buried their own recording. Unsurprisingly, the single bombed, creeping to Number 87 on the Billboard chart.

At the very end of the track on the album is a period of snoring. This was apparently actually Wyman who had fallen asleep in the studio and was recorded covertly by Jagger and Richards, and he was unaware of its presence until he heard the finished album. The snoring is edited off the single, not that it helped...

'2000 Man' (Jagger / Richards)

It's kind of strange to hear this song now, with Jagger singing about the '2000 Man' as if it is in a distant sci-fi vision of the future. Perhaps he might have been advised to set it more than 33 years in the future – although we of a certain age will remember only too well the idea that it would be all flying cars and moving pavements in 'the year 2000'. Nonetheless, lyrical timescale aside, this is an infectious and enjoyable track. It begins with an acoustic guitar intro from Richards with Nicky Hopkins on piano and possibly Jones on what sounds like some kind of dulcimer. Jagger comes in with the first couple of verses, digging out all of the standard science fiction tropes such as his name being a number, and having an affair with a 'random computer', etc. Why he doesn't choose a specific computer we are not told. At the same time Watts joins in with a far too busy drum pattern which doesn't help the flow. Anyhow, this jaunty country-folk section skips along for a minute and a half or so, with an especially engaging chorus, before it abruptly changes into a much rockier mid-section featuring endless repetition of the somewhat random phrase 'Oh daddy, proud of your planet / Oh mummy, proud of your sun'. Leaving aside the lyrical banality of this section, it is actually the best part of the song, building up a fair head of steam before the track reverts to the opening section again in slightly rocked-up style to play out. Overall, it is far too haphazardly constructed to be truly effective, yet it is undeniably enjoyable for all its flaws.

A decade later American rock band Kiss included a cover of the track on their album *Dynasty*. Sung by guitarist Ace Frehley, this version is considered by many as superior to the original, yet oddly enough the heavy rock treatment works best in the opening section, getting a little bit lost in the middle part, which was the rocker element of the Stones' version.

'Sing This All Together (See What Happens)' (Jagger, Richards)

Well, just in case anyone thought the opening song on the album was too safe, here it is again as the inspiration behind an eight-and-a-half minute extrapolation which is so far out it's practically on its way in again at the other door ... this is genuinely ground-breaking stuff even for the time. Opening with brief snippets of conversation, culminating in what sounds like Jagger asking, 'Where's that joint?', we are led through an aural soundscape of bizarre yet hypnotic allure. The refrain from 'Sing This All Together' gives a sort of starting point before emerging in its full form after seven minutes of chaos. After this the track devolves into a final 30 seconds of sound collage which, if speeded up, can be heard to be the melody of 'We Wish You A Merry Christmas', being a reference to the original album title, Cosmic Christmas. This track pre-empts what space-rock bands like Hawkwind were doing sometime later only in much more home-made fashion, and it is a fascinating listen. It really shouldn't hang together, but amazingly it does.

'She's A Rainbow' (Jagger, Richards)

Another track released as a US single (though not in the UK, where the charts were presumably judged not to be ready for this stuff), the exuberant 'She's A Rainbow' has long been held up as one of the most successful, and certainly most commercial, tracks on the album. The track opens with the sound of a carnival sideshow barker calling people to play his game, and select any prize, pick of the stall, etc., before the song enters, borne on Hopkins' piano. The structure is unusual, in that we get a couple of choruses with instrumental sections where the verses would be until around midway through, when Jagger begins singing the verses. The lyrical content, about the unidentified woman who is the beautiful subject of the song, is unashamedly pop-psychedelia, and overall the track is the only Stones song which could easily fit onto a 'Summer of Love' compilation album, alongside standards like 'San Francisco' and 'A Whiter Shade of Pale'. In this regard, it seems rather odd that the single was not released in the UK – it reached Number 25 in the US, but such was the slightly belated appetite for anything psychedelic in tone in the UK by the end of '67 that it could easily have performed much better than that. Note that the fairground intro section was omitted from the single.

The impressive string arrangements used on the track were put together by none other than John Paul Jones, later of Led Zeppelin, who had been working for Decca for a couple of years by that time. These strings add greatly to the song, and on close listening can be heard to echo the styles of a number of different composers, including Mozart and Bartok, during the track.

'The Lantern' (Jagger, Richards)

This is a genuinely overlooked and often misunderstood song in the Stones catalogue. Often dismissed – when mentioned at all – as some kind of unfocused hippy novelty, it is actually a tremendously cleverly constructed track which carries a profound lyrical punch. The protagonist of the song is a man whose lover / soulmate / wife (whatever you will) has passed away before him. Whilst they were alive, they have clearly made a pact that when it is his turn to die, she will come to him and they will be able to communicate across the 'veil' by the mysterious lantern of the title. One night, this comes to pass as the man (who is seemingly a rich man or a lord, going by the mention of the servants) finds himself with his face turning 'a deathly pale' as she visits him once again carrying the 'lantern light', whereupon, unnoticed by anyone else, his heart stops as he goes with her, beseeching her to 'carry the lantern high'. This is deep and moving lyrical territory, and is brilliantly matched by the music, in which Richards and Hopkins manage to incorporate blues guitar and some boogie piano into a whole which nonetheless has the effect of being sombre and, without doubt, proto-progressive rock. This is a great, forgotten piece which surely deserves its moment in the sun.

'Gomper' (Jagger, Richards)

Ah yes, the inevitable 'Stones go Indian' moment. Seemingly de rigueur for any self-respecting psychedelic experimentalist in 1967, and given Jones' experimentation with the sitar previously on 'Paint It Black' this was always likely to happen. In truth, it's hard work. The song starts off as a straightforward enough psychedelic drone, with Jagger eulogising about a woman he has 'observed' emerging from a lake with lily flowers one evening, to dry off naked in the sun. He 'stifles a cry', we hear. I'll bet he did.

Following that bit of lysergically approved voyeurism, when the track gets towards the two-minute mark, we get the abrupt shift into an Indian inspired improvisation for the following, rather laboured three minutes. I say 'Indian inspired' because whereas the Beatles had a genuinely serious Indian music student in George Harrison, the Stones had to make do with a stash of LSD and Brian Jones, who may have been enthusiastic but was already beginning to wander away with the fairies by this time. It noodles along okay, and its heart is in the right place, but it really is Amateur Hour. The title is most odd. 'Gomper' is a slang, derisory word for an utterly stupid individual, but the song's working titles of 'Flowers in Your Hair' or 'The Ladies, The Lilies and The Lake' would surely have been more fitting. Unless the 'gomper' of the title was the leering voyeur by the lake, or even an in-joke at the band's clueless approach to Indian music, there seems little to shed light on it.

'2000 Light Years from Home' (Jagger, Richards)

Along with 'She's A Rainbow', this cosmic tale of intergalactic loneliness is easily the most celebrated track on the album – and indeed was the other side of the 'She's A Rainbow' single. A tale of the prolonged journey of an astronaut to Aldebaran, and the solitude and loneliness he falls prey to, the music perfectly matches the lyric. At each refrain, when he is a hundred, then six hundred, then a thousand and finally two thousand light years from home, his voice tails away and the spacey background evokes the darkness and emptiness of deep space with chilling effectiveness. With Richards' insistent and repetitive guitar riffing and Watts' hypnotic drum pattern supported by Jones' other-worldly Mellotron and Wyman's oscillator, this track is grossly undervalued in its contribution to the birth of what became progressive rock. The space-rock favoured by Hawkwind and their ilk effectively began in 1967 with two tracks: this one and Pink Floyd's 'Interstellar Overdrive'. Scandalously, one is lauded as Syd Barrett's genius while the other is largely written off as the Stones 'going through a phase'. While it is true that they soon pulled back from this direction, their contribution should not be understated. Incidentally, the odd effect at the beginning of the track is produced by Hopkins striking and plucking the strings of the piano inside the instrument itself, a rather similar technique to that used by Keith Emerson during the mid-section of 'Take A Pebble' some three years later.

The powerfully evocative lyrics were actually written by Jagger in his cell at Brixton Jail, the night before he was released on bail. With no idea that he would be freed the next day, he was seized by a profound feeling of loneliness and used the lyric to express the feeling in an oblique way, something which really became masterfully clear once it was added to the melting pot of the music.

'On with the Show' (Jagger, Richards)

A real surprise to close the album, as the psychedelia and experimentation cease abruptly to be replaced by a sort of vaudevillian atmosphere, closer to the closing tracks on each side of *Between the Buttons* than the weighty acid-drenched experimentation of what has gone before. Clearly set in the surroundings of a seedy yet faux-genteel strip club, Jagger comes across as the

Master of Ceremonies, describing the delights on offer for the delectation of the patrons, through what sounds like a megaphone, and ending each verse with a toast of 'On with the show, Good health to you!' in a plummy, BBC Home Service sort of voice. It's nothing of any great significance or magnitude, yet it is an oddly charming way to close the album, leaving a smile on the face of the listener. There would be a big difference next time out for sure, but *Satanic Majesties* still stands as an enormously enjoyable 40 minutes or so of music, and the band's most underrated album.

Related Songs:

'Jumpin' Jack Flash' (Jagger, Richards)

If you want to pin down one pivotal moment when the career and importance of the Rolling Stones instantly and permanently shifted, this song would be it. Released in July 1968, six months before the *Beggars Banquet* album for which it was originally earmarked, the last remnant of any fey psychedelia left around from the previous couple of years is scorched away by this incendiary blues-rock monster. Opening with some propulsive and scything guitar chords, Jagger's terse 'Watch it!' leads into a swaggering, imperious Richards riff which simply defines the Stones at this point and thereafter. Everything is in here: the real beginning of the band's louche swagger which led to them being described as 'the greatest rock and roll band in the world', Jagger's assumption of his dark, almost satanic character and Richards' trademark habit of tossing guitar riffs off like so much confetti with seemingly effortless abandon. And you can dance to it!

Few opening lines can be as iconic as 'I was born in a crossfire hurricane', and the song goes on to deliver a list of similar catastrophic occurrences, such as being raised by a toothless bearded hag, drowned, washed up and left for dead, and finally crowned with a spike right through his head. Some of this appears Christ-like in imagery (the crown of thorns reference in that last line, and also the crucifixion feel of 'I fell down to my feet and I saw they bled'), while others simply appear to refer to a hard life ('I was schooled with a strap right across my back', etc). Ultimately, it doesn't matter who or what this character is meant to be. All that does matter is the fact that the lyrical intensity and casual, yet incendiary, musical maelstrom come together in a perfect synergy to post an image of Jagger and the Stones in people's minds which was as strong as it was ultimately indescribable. They were The Stones, they were, at that time, The Most Dangerous Band in The World and a long way from their early, simplistic 'long-haired and scruffy' personas. It was only rock and roll. But they liked it.

One surprising thing about the song is that almost all of the guitars you hear are acoustic. Jones contributes some electric rhythm guitar, but all of Richards' lead parts and that main riff are played on an acoustic guitar straight into the microphone which came with Richards' new Philips cassette recorder, an effect which overloaded it and made it function almost – as Keith himself put it – as an amp and pre-amp rolled into one. It made acoustic seem electric, yet still with the open expansiveness that came with it. Bill Wyman (who is on organ on the track, with Richards handling bass duties) claims in his autobiography to have come up with the basic riff on the keyboard originally, and that he should have received a writing credit. It is very probable that he has a case, but what cannot ultimately be denied is that Richards took the basic tools and forged them in the crucible of his own experimentation and skewed genius to turn base metal into gold. Rolled Gold.

The song soared straight to Number One in the UK as soon as it was released. Of course, it did. The US Billboard chart was a little slower to respond, with the single peaking at Number Three, but the world soon caught up. The song is the most-played in concert of all Stones compositions, featuring in every single tour from 1968 to the present day, and numbering over 1100 performances. And every time, it's a gas.

'Child of The Moon' (Jagger, Richards)

The B-side to 'Jumpin' Jack Flash', this unfairly obscure song manages to place a foot in two camps: begun during the *Satanic Majesties* sessions, it certainly has the densely interpretive lyrics and creepy psychedelic sound to fit on that album, yet its construction is equally cut from the country-blues/rock territory which the Stones were on their way to. Many have called the song an ode to Marianne Faithfull, and the three verses do indeed appear to address an unspecified yet almost mystical female presence, but there are lyrical allusions to symbology from the Sun and Moon, mist and fog, through to 'the end of the highway', which suggests something darker. If not a woman, who is the mysterious child of the Moon? Jagger himself is almost a Moonchild astrologically but misses by a few days.

The darker interpretation is borne out by the promotional film, directed by Michael Lindsay-Hogg – later to be the man behind the ill-fated Rock and Roll Circus production – in a surprising move for a mere B-side. The film depicts a child, a young-ish woman and an elderly woman all emerging from the same dark wood onto a road with their way blocked by the silent figures of the five Stones (although Jones, who had disappeared during the shoot in his deteriorating state, is only seen looking out from behind a tree). The impression is clearly that the three figures are the same woman in different stages of her life, while the band appear to represent some kind of sentinels of the afterlife. The young girl, playing with a ball, looks at them, laughs, and leaves in a carefree fashion as if it is irrelevant to her at this stage. The middle-aged woman, who looks careworn and troubled, approaches them but is blocked from proceeding, including by Keith who swings down nimbly from a high tree branch; she ultimately retreats, as if persuaded that she should not yet end her life. When she returns as an old woman, she approaches the figures and brushes past Jagger, who steps aside for her, as she walks beyond them to a waiting white horse. It is a quite brilliant piece of film-making and, once seen, is forever associated with the song in the listener's head.

The production of the track (like 'Jack Flash' it marks the beginning of the Stones' work with producer Jimmy Miller) lends a droning air reminiscent of the Beatles' 'Rain' via Watts' hypnotic drums and Jones' background Saxophone particularly. Miller is also responsible for the eerie and largely indecipherable snatch of speech buried in the introduction. Jones plays nothing else on the song, and he is looking more and more disconnected. He reportedly pleaded for the track to be the A-side, with 'Jack Flash' relegated to the B-side. It's a good song, but let's face it, that was never going to happen.

Beggars Banquet (1968)

Personnel:
Mick Jagger: vocals, harmonics, percussion
Keith Richards: guitar, vocals, bass
Brian Jones: guitar, harmonica, Mellotron, sitar, tambura, backing vocals
Bill Wyman: bass, vocals, synthesizer, percussion
Charlie Watts: drums and percussion, backing vocals
With
Nicky Hopkins: piano, Mellotron
Rocky Dijon: congas
Ric Grech: violin
Dave Mason: Shehnai

Record Label: Decca (UK), London (US)
Recorded: March-July 196, produced by Jimmy Miller
Release Date: December 1968.
Highest chart places: UK: 3, US: 5
Running time: 39:44

Album Facts:

Apart from its generally received wisdom as one of the band's finest albums, and the start of the widely accepted 'golden run' of albums across the next few years, *Beggars Banquet* (note, no apostrophe) was notable for two things. Firstly, the stripping back of the sound to more of a country/blues influence again, effectively turning the Stones right back to a rock and roll band once more, but also the considerable withdrawal of Brian Jones from the recording process.

Jones was cutting an increasingly worrying figure, strung out on various narcotics, haunted by paranoia and depression rooted in police harassment and Anita Pallenberg's defection to Richards, and crucially losing interest in the creative force within the Stones. According to producer Jimmy Miller, Jones would fail to show up at the studio for significant periods, finally arriving when he felt like playing, sometimes with an instrument totally unsuitable for what the band were working on (such as a sitar for a blues session). At such times Miller was encouraged by the rest of the band to try to keep Jones out of the way for the sake of their work, and he was sometimes recorded in a booth for no intended purpose on whatever instrument he had brought along. Richards said later that things had got to a point where they were relieved if he was absent because it meant the rest of them could get on with their work. In the end, Jones contributed to only six of the album's ten tracks, often fairly marginally, which is sad when one considers that when he was, infrequently, still in the 'zone', his musical genius could still light up the sessions. His slide guitar work on the track 'No Expectations' was the best example of this, but apart from that he scarcely picked up a guitar, with Richards becoming the chief architect of the band's sound. *Beggars Banquet* was the last Stones album to be released while Jones was still alive.

The album title was reportedly suggested by the art and antiquities dealer and interior design guru Christopher Gibbs, who was working on the decoration of Jagger's Chelsea flat.

Album Cover:

For a while, the saga of the intended album cover for the record was threatening to overshadow the music itself. Mick and Keith had come upon a rather insalubrious public toilet in Los Angeles with a rather graphically graffiti-adorned wall, and they were much taken with the image. They had it photographed by Barry Feinstein – after a few pertinent additions were added to it, referencing the album – and showed the photo to the powers that be at Decca back in London. These powers promptly put their collective feet down and announced that there was no way on this earth that such 'poor taste' would go anywhere near the cover of one of their label's releases. London Records in the US were on this occasion rather less demanding, insisting only that extra graffiti with the band name and album title were added for marketing purposes! A stand-off developed between the band on one side and the Decca arbiters of taste on the other. During one particularly celebrated exchange between Jagger and Decca chief Sir Edward Lewis, when the latter accused the cover of being in poor taste, the singer replied, some would say not unreasonably, that he found it rather more upsetting that Decca had recently released an album by Tom Jones (*A-Tom-Ic Jones*) which featured an atom bomb exploding on the front cover! He also added later, with a touch of knowing humour, that they had tried to keep it within the bounds of good taste, adding 'I mean, we haven't shown the whole lavatory!'

Such entreaties were fruitless as Lewis and his team refused to budge, and after a significant delay beyond the hoped-for late Summer release, the album eventually emerged on 6 December 1968 with a gatefold sleeve in the form of a large invitation, with 'The Rolling Stones' and 'Beggars Banquet' in flowing script and 'RSVP' in the corner. The rear featured the track names and credits in the same scholarly hand, while the inner gatefold consisted of a photo taken at a neo-Tudor manor house in Hampstead named Sarum Chase, at a photo session back in June; depicting the banquet itself, it shows the five Stones in debauched fashion and beggars' attire, enjoying the pleasures of an opulently stocked table. There are oddities about the photo: firstly, it is strangely tinted and effectively monochrome apart from the band members' faces and skin, and secondly they are accompanied by several animals – not so unusual in terms of a cat and a large dog, and even what may be a monkey, but certainly more so in terms of a sheep standing on a flight of stairs...

'Sympathy for the Devil' (Jagger, Richards)

If 'Jumpin' Jack Flash' was the track which introduced the malevolent, Mephistophelean image of Jagger (and by extension, the Stones) in the public eye, 'Sympathy for the Devil' was the moment which crystallised the impression and sealed it forever in amber. Almost entirely written by Jagger, his was the basic musical idea, with Richards effectively helping him find the best tempo and arrangement and polishing the end result.

Taking the lyrics first, as one feels obliged to with a work of this substantial magnitude, 'Sympathy for the Devil' not only works as prose or poetry on its own but is, without doubt, one of the most erudite, literary and thought-provoking lyrics in all of popular music. Opening with the timeless 'Please allow me to introduce myself, I'm a man of wealth and taste' greeting by Satan himself, the lyric goes on to list the historical catastrophes and acts of evil with an almost lip-smacking relish, while turning ideas of moral and religious doctrines on their heads ('Just as every cop is a criminal / And all the sinners saints / As heads is tails just call me Lucifer'). Events alluded to include the crucifixion, the Hundred Years War, the Second World War, the Russian Revolution and the assassination of JFK. The line about laying 'traps for troubadours / Who get killed before they reach Bombay' may be a reference to the pre-Colonial 'Thuggee' cult who waylaid and murdered travellers, though the 'troubadours' use is sometimes claimed to be regarding hippie travellers who headed to India in the metaphorical footsteps of the Beatles. The exact details are not as important as the overall impression, however, and the depiction of the Devil as a well-spoken socialite. It is believed that Jagger got the inspiration for the song from the Russian novel The Master and Margarita, by Mikhail Bulgakov, which concerns the arrival of the Devil in 1930s Moscow and portrays him as 'a man of wealth and taste' – he had recently read the book at the suggestion of Marianne Faithfull. One final thing to note about the lyric is that the line 'I shouted out, "Who killed the Kennedys?"' originally referred only to John F. Kennedy but was changed after Robert Kennedy was himself killed during the time of recording sessions.

Of course, a great lyric can only get you so far, and thankfully, in this case, the music is equally masterful. Beginning, as Mick and Keith both recall, as a 'sort of folk song', it was transformed into a dynamic, insistent Samba rhythm, an unexpected tactic which works brilliantly. Coming in on percussion alone, Jagger soon enters along with a bedrock of piano from Nicky Hopkins, and over the course of the verses the track builds in intensity with more and more layers of percussion entering the fray along with a fat, thrumming bass line courtesy of Keith (Wyman is on percussion duties on this one). Jagger delivers a vocal masterclass here, moving from seductive sections where his voice positively drips with honeyed malevolence to dramatic, insistent declamations of the Devil's trail over the years, with the finger being pointed at Man for seemingly being complicit by his own inaction. It's one of the great song deliveries, and the accompaniment almost gives a voodoo-like trance feel to the whole thing. Keith rips off a searing solo before the song proper comes back in for its dramatic vocal conclusion. By this point, a host of people, including most of the band and a brilliant conga performance throughout by guest

Rocky Dijon, are all providing a wall of percussion without any need for Watts to touch his actual drumkit. As the coda to the song thunders on with Keith peeling off electric licks like a wizard producing sparks from his fingertips, a distinctive 'woo-woo' vocal backing is provided by band, girlfriends and producer Jimmy Miller, all gathered together. The overall effect leaves the listener almost breathless, and it is surely one of the greatest album openers of all time, and for 1968 it was utterly ground-breaking.

So heavily did the spirit of dark mysticism hang over this song that, after the murder at the infamous Altamont Speedway concert the following year, the band did not perform the song live in concert for seven years. In truth, the band were playing 'Under My Thumb' when the stabbing of Meredith Hunter took place by the stage, but urban legend has often suggested it was indeed this song. The Jean-Luc Goddard film One Plus One (later retitled Sympathy for the Devil) depicts the evolution of the song throughout the recording sessions, juxtaposed with surreal accompanying real-life footage, and is a fascinating document – poignantly showing a weary-looking Brian Jones at one point, playing acoustic guitar which was never even made audible in the final result.

'No Expectations' (Jagger, Richards)

This beautiful, mournful country-blues ballad displays, as the band have attested, the last truly meaningful contribution of Brian Jones to the band, as he overlays the song with some superbly nuanced acoustic slide guitar work. Richards' chord progression is heartbreakingly forlorn, with Wyman's subtly sympathetic bass runs and Hopkins' lovely piano from around halfway in putting the icing on this tremendous musical cake. Jagger delivers the tale of the lovelorn protagonist left with 'no expectations to pass this way again' with just the right level of sentimentality – stopping just short of overdoing it and in the process conjuring a devastatingly sorrowful effect. With this almost becoming a tribute to Jones after his death the following year, it becomes almost unbearably tragic. Anyone who has ever claimed the Stones could not do tenderness should start here.

'Dear Doctor' (Jagger, Richards)

A real change of mood here for this hilarious drunken country pastiche set in the American South, which sees the band loosely stumble through the backing as Jagger relates a tale of a wedding doomed to failure, but which we quickly find he has been dreading and thus 'soaking up drink like a sponge'. Indeed, the song begins with him appealing to the doctor to take out his pained heart and 'preserve it right there in that jar', but we see that it is the thought of the nuptials to his intended 'bow-legged sow' that devastates him so, as his mother forces him into it. However, salvation arrives as, just before the ceremony, he finds a note in his jacket pocket from his betrothed, informing him (in a riotous Jagger impersonation) that she is in Virginia with his cousin Lou, and that the wedding is off. In joyful relief, he tells the doctor he can replace his heart again as his 'pulse is now under control'. A great musical statement this is not, but it is enormous fun, which is really all it aspires to. And what's wrong with that?

'Parachute Woman' (Jagger, Richards)

A much heavier and aggressive blues track here, with lyrics celebrating the groupie contingent of the USA, with – let's be honest – barely veiled innuendo! Jagger is at his lascivious best with his litany of 'acquaintances', while Richards sounds soaked in the swamp-blues spirit as he accompanies him on the electric guitar. Amazingly, four songs in, this is the first song on the album to feature an actual drumkit as opposed to other forms of percussion! The harmonica, particularly the concluding solo section, is generally believed from its style to be courtesy of Jagger rather than Jones. This track is one of those illustrated in graffiti on the 'toilet wall' sleeve design, in fairly graphic fashion. Once again, it has no pretensions to be anything other than what it is, which is a stinging, rollicking blues-rock workout taking the band right back to their pre-psychedelia roots.

'Jigsaw Puzzle' (Jagger, Richards)

A real underrated gem on the album, and indeed in the history of the Stones, this six-minute opus takes us right back into Dylan territory again – and specifically his wordy, rambling yet hypnotic *Blonde on Blonde* era. Beginning in very stark fashion, the song gains more and more momentum and vitality as it goes on, gaining instrumentation as it goes. Jagger's fascinating lyric introduces a litany of classically Dylan-esque characters (the tramp, the bishop's daughter, the gangster) before taking the listener through a verse referencing the whole band and finally ending with some English social commentary via the 'twenty thousand grandmas' waving their hankies in the air while 'burning up their pensions' in some protest. And all the while, as the choruses tell us, Jagger is simply trying to do his jigsaw puzzle 'before it rains any more'. Somehow, we feel he will never manage it, and that the puzzle is a kind of metaphor for the unfathomable chaos of life which we can't control – there's always more 'rain' around the corner. Very fertile scope for imagination is laid out in the words, which also manage that Dylan trick of sounding so good together that the meaning is almost unimportant. Not an easy trick to pull off, but it's done so well here. Richards excels on electric, acoustic and slide guitar, Watts propels the song irresistibly while Jagger is again on great vocal form, revelling in a classic opportunity to engage in his 'vocal acting' that Loog Oldham referred to years before, while also singing extremely well. There is a consistent 'whine' backing the music on a couple of occasions mid-way through and at the conclusion, which is often credited to Jones, either on Mellotron or a heavily reverb-laden dulcimer. The band have never played this song live, which is a shame. If nothing else, the verse going through the band members would generate some tremendous crowd reaction, one imagines.

'The guitar players look damaged / They've been outcasts all their lives'. Well, quite ...

'Street Fighting Man' (Jagger, Richards)

In terms of defining *Beggars Banquet* as a subversive release, branding the Stones forever as 'lords of misrule', 'Street Fighting Man' is the twin peak alongside 'Sympathy for the Devil'. Released in the US as the first single from the album (oddly, it did not get a UK single release until some three years later), it was summarily banned by many of the more cautious – some would say paranoid – US radio stations. In truth, such a reaction was disproportionate – both from the media and also the general public, who have now become convinced almost en masse that if they weren't actually agents of Satan, then that nasty Mr Jagger and his unkempt friends were certainly going to invade their streets and leave us cowering inside their homes. All of this was a nonsense to anyone who had actually listened properly to the song, as to a large degree it has Jagger bemoaning, via another razor-sharp lyric, that such social unrest as was happening in France and the USA at the time in 1968 was never likely to happen in the rather more sedate UK, where there is 'just no place for a street fighting man', and the prevailing game is of 'compromise solution'.

Musically, for such a strident rocker, this is another surprise in the mould of 'Jumpin' Jack Flash' in that all of the guitars heard are acoustic, Keith pulling off that great trick with the overdriven cassette recorder microphone again. It certainly sounds like no acoustic guitar you would ever imagine, with its aggressive and staccato riffing driving along Jagger's equally propulsive vocal (which really does evoke 'marching, charging feet' in the verses). The choruses explode in an almost euphoric burst as Jagger lets loose with the classic 'Well what can a poor boy do / 'Cept to sing for a rock and roll band' couplet, and the die is cast for another Stones classic. Jones can be heard on this, droning away with a surprisingly fitting sitar part, and from the last chorus at a little over two minutes, Hopkins comes in with some superb piano. Bill Wyman plays no part on this recording, but Traffic's guitarist Dave Mason does contribute some percussion and shehnai (an Asian woodwind instrument). Watts, bizarrely, plays his whole part on the track using a 1930s toy drum kit called a 'London Jazz Kit', largely because he could get really close to Keith's overdriven acoustic guitar, physically speaking. The music was written first by some margin, but the all-important lyric was conceived by Jagger after he attended a London anti-Vietnam rally in early 1968; it was undoubtedly a day well spent!

'Prodigal Son' (Wilkins)

Pure blues here, as the Stones attempt a cover version on an album for the first time since *Out of Our Heads* with this song written by bluesman Robert

Wilkins. It's simple and does effectively what it says on the tin: a Stones cover of a straight, if upbeat, blues song which tells the well-worn story of the Prodigal Son, updated for depression-era dustbowl America. Wilkins was a fascinating character: witnessing a murder in 1936, when he was 40, he quit playing the blues and joined the Church soon afterwards. In 1950, when he was 54, he was ordained and became 'The Rev Robert Wilkins', his stage name when he was rediscovered by a contemporary audience and began playing festivals, etc. There is no bass on the recording, and there have been reports that Ry Cooder can be heard on acoustic guitar during the take, but there has been no verification of this. On early copies of the album, the song is mistakenly credited to 'Jagger / Richards', but this was later re-credited.

'Stray Cat Blues' (Jagger, Richards)

On which the Stones once again fail to endear themselves to the middle-class, conservatively-valued public – they might not be satanic or street-fighting on this track, but they sure were out to defile your daughters. Hmm, yeah!

Jagger is at his libidinous best here on this 'targeted to shock' piece detailing encounters with, once again, groupies out on the road – only this time in the form of a clearly far from virtuous fifteen year old girl (not to mention her friend, who gets invited 'upstairs' near the end for a threesome!). Jagger is loving this role, and he spits out lines like 'There'll be a feast if you just come upstairs' and 'Bet your mama don't know you can scratch like that' with obvious relish. There's even a line which says 'No, I don't want your ID', for heaven's sake! In concert on the 1968 tour, immortalised on the *Get Yer Ya-Ya's Out* album, he actually tested his audience's reaction by reducing the age of the girl in question to thirteen!

'It ain't no hanging matter', he crows confidently, 'It ain't no capital crime'. Well, maybe not a capital crime, but let's just say this track would probably not have got a release today. Let's just take a moment to consider what this album's release says about Britain in 1968: openly admitted underage sex? 'Okay chaps, that's fine. After all, this IS the new permissive society!' Graffiti on a toilet wall? 'What? Are you insane? No, we will block this for months, you band of degenerates!' Different times, very different times. Great rock track though, with some tremendous piano from the terribly underrated Hopkins. Towards the end there is an almost jazzy breakdown, carried with just some bass and then drums, which leads into a final instrumental section. Jagger has asserted that the band were very influenced by 'Heroin' by the Velvet Underground when recording and writing this track, and there is certainly some similarity.

'Factory Girl' (Jagger, Richards)

A pure country song in style and execution, this brief two-minute number is paradoxically utterly English in its lyrical content. The scenario has Jagger waiting outside the factory for his girl to finish her shift, and it is painted like a typical 1960s 'kitchen sink drama', as cleverly chosen words introduce us

Above: October 1963 concert flyer for Cardiff, on a strong bill with the Everley Brothers and Bo Diddley (oddly dressed as a Cowboy). Note they're still promoting 'Come On.' *(Matt Lee)*

Right: A 1964 US magazine. It's an awkward cover pose, to say the least, with Keith's acoustic guitar in a seemingly impossible playing position, and Mick resembling a waxwork. *(Curt Angeledes)*

LEFT: The UK cover of the self-titled debut album, released in 1964. The US cover was the same but added the band name plus *England's Newest Hit Makers*, which bizarrely became adopted as the official title. *(Decca Records)*

RIGHT: *12x5*, which was a US-only album, featuring a mixture of tracks from UK albums, plus singles. The cover is the same photo as the UK *Rolling Stones No 2*. *(London Records)*

LEFT: The cover of the 1965 US-only album *The Rolling Stones Now!* It followed soon after *12x5*. The track listings and cover designs differed extensively between the US and the UK until 1966, and gets rather confusing at this time! *(London Records)*

RIGHT: The US version of *Out Of Our Heads*, which differed greatly in track listing from the UK release of the same title, and also used an entirely different cover design *(London Records)*

LEFT: Another US only album in the form of *December's Children (And Everybody's)*. Note that the cover design this time out is the same as that first used on the UK pressing of *Out Of Our Heads*! Confused? Don't feel bad; everybody was! *(London Records)*

RIGHT: The *Aftermath* US release. Again, this is a different track listing and cover design to the UK release. This US design was widely felt to be a better fit, but I'm not so sure. Good news, though - this was the last album to be released with different cover designs on the two sides of the Atlantic! *(London Records)*

Albert A. Bonici and Andy Lothian, Jnr. present

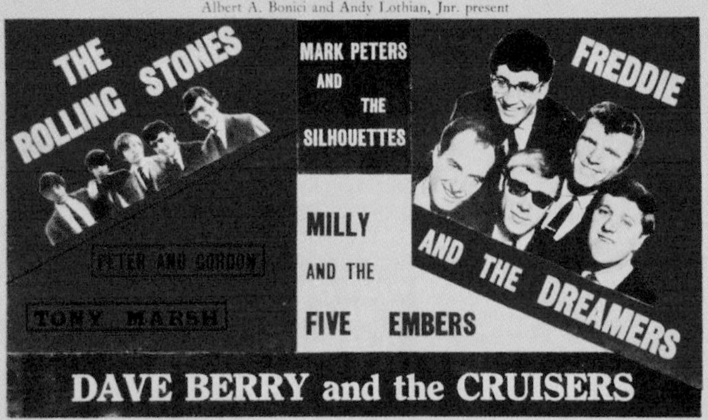

Above: A May 1964 concert flyer for a doubleheader with the not-so-mighty Freddie And The Dreamers, at an unspecified Capitol cinema. All these early bills had seven bands and two shows, which defies belief as to how short their sets were, and how quickly they must have been shuttled on and off stage. *(Matt Lee)*

Left: A March 1965 concert flyer for the grand setting of the ABC, Huddersfield. The Stones were clearly headlining by now though, even over the Hollies *(Matt Lee)*

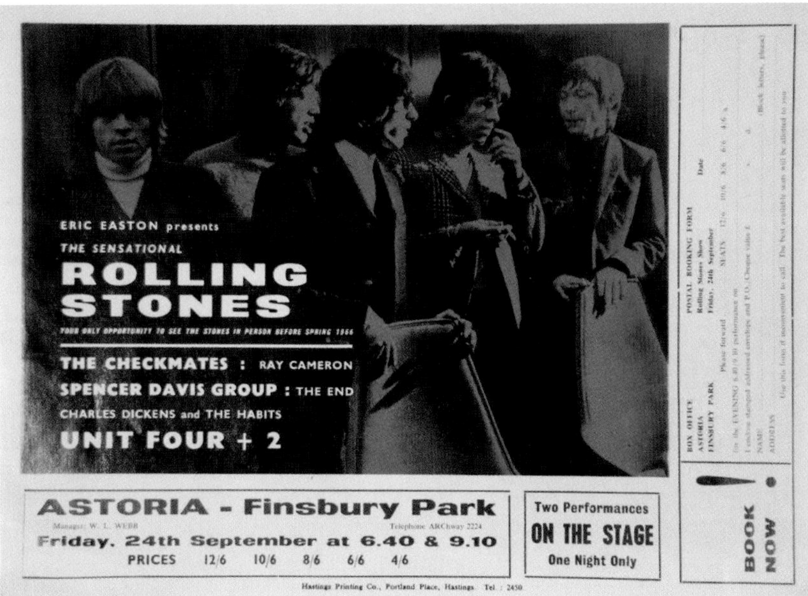

Above: A September 1965 concert flyer for another variety bill, at Finsbury Park Astoria. The Stones are now well and truly the top draw, with The Spencer Davis Group and Unit 4+2 reduced to small lettering along with other acts who have faded into obscurity *(Matt Lee)*

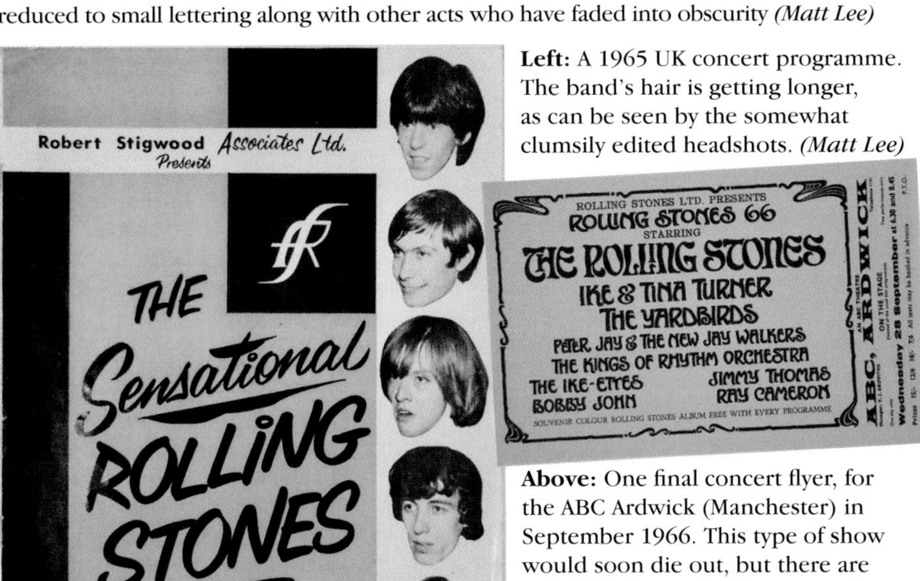

Left: A 1965 UK concert programme. The band's hair is getting longer, as can be seen by the somewhat clumsily edited headshots. *(Matt Lee)*

Above: One final concert flyer, for the ABC Ardwick (Manchester) in September 1966. This type of show would soon die out, but there are nine bands here. The design and font have become much more 'psychedelic' as 1967 approaches, while Ike and Tina Turner and the Yardbirds make up a strong bill. *(Matt Lee)*

LEFT: The *Between The Buttons* album cover. There were track listing differences here between the UK and US, but at least the title and cover design were identical now. *(Decca Records)*

RIGHT: The *Their Satanic Majesties Request* album cover. It was the first album to have no differences between the UK and US. Early pressings of this had the questionably exotic cover photo as lenticular 3D art. *(Decca Records)*

LEFT: The *Beggars Banquet* original front cover from 1968, after the 'graffiti cover' was banned. This cover was the official one for decades, into the CD age, and while it is less provocative, the RSVP gatefold 'invitation' does have a certain elegance, with the actual 'banquet' shown inside. *(Decca Records)*

RIGHT: The *Beggars Banquet* banned 'graffiti' cover, finally abandoned after months of wrangling between Jagger and Decca. For the next three decades this was a source of fascination, only reproduced occasionally in books. It all seems rather tame now. *(Decca Records)*

LEFT: The *Let It Bleed* album cover, featuring a cake by a young Delia Smith, for one of her first baking commissions. The band is atop the cake with Brian Jones, who died during July 1969, represented rather than new boy Mick Taylor. *(Decca Records)*

RIGHT: The Sticky Fingers album cover from 1971, with the infamous working zip - a scourge of many an adjoining album in record collections (and shops) around the world. Inside the zip was hidden a rather unappealing photograph of some underpants. *(Rolling Stones Records)*

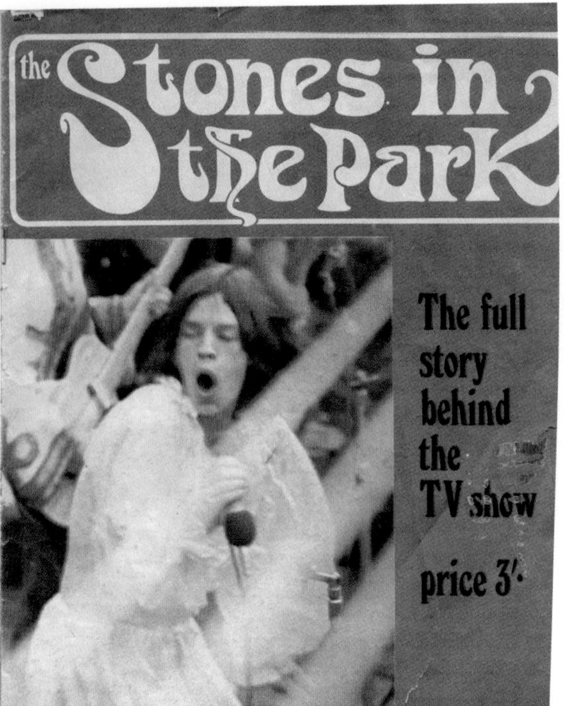

Left: A Souvenir brochure commemorating the 1969 Hyde Park free concert, put out shortly after the event when it received a TV broadcast.
(Gudbjorg Ogmundsdottir)

Right: A page from the Hyde Park brochure, showing Jagger and Taylor calmly seated as far more excited audience members climb up the stage front.
(Gudbjorg Ogmundsdottir)

Above: Mick Jagger onstage at Hyde Park during a performance of 'Satisfaction' later in the show after he had discarded his somewhat foppish white blouse-style shirt.

Right: Another page from the aforementioned Hyde Park brochure, showing individual shots of the band, presumably taken backstage.
(Gudbjorg Ogmundsdottir)

LEFT: The very literal Spanish cover to *Sticky Fingers*. Somehow, severed fingers emerging from a tin of treacle were deemed more acceptable than a pair of jeans, for this release, which also excised the controversial 'Sister Morphine' in favour of a live version of 'Let It Rock.'.
(Rolling Stones Records)

RIGHT: The 1970 European Tour poster, with a rather 'art deco' feel to it.
(Matt Lee)

Right: The 1973 European Tour poster, with a rather cleverly designed use of a female model. Only five years earlier, a toilet wall had been banned. The world had really moved on. *(Matt Lee)*

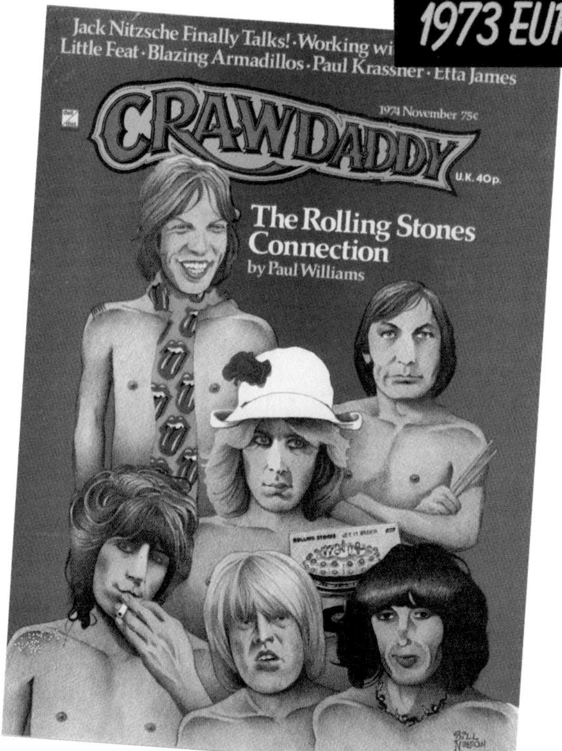

Left: *Crawdaddy* magazine cover from 1974. Note the terrible cartoon representation of the band! Somehow, this artwork must have been commissioned and accepted. Still, it WAS the '70s. *(Curt Angeledes)*

Above: Ronnie, Mick, and Keith, onstage at Jacksonville, Florida, USA, on the 'Tour Of The Americas,' 1975. *(Curt Angeledes)*

Right: Onstage in 1975 in Philadelphia, Pennsylvania, USA. Note Ian Stewart on piano in the background - he and Billy Preston both accompanied the Stones on this tour. *(Curt Angeledes)*

Above: The real Memory Motel in Montauk, NY, which inspired, and gave its name to, the song. The band was rehearsing for the 1975 US tour nearby at Andy Warhol's house when the song was first conceived. *(Glenn Michael Schneider - www.glennschneiderstudios.com)*

Left: The US Tour poster for the *Some Girls* tour, 1978. In a strange choice of artwork, the band pay homage to Soviet poster design. Despite the somewhat tangential relevance to *Some Girls*, the artwork nevertheless received a second life decades later as the cover art for a live CD and DVD from this tour.. *(Matt Lee)*

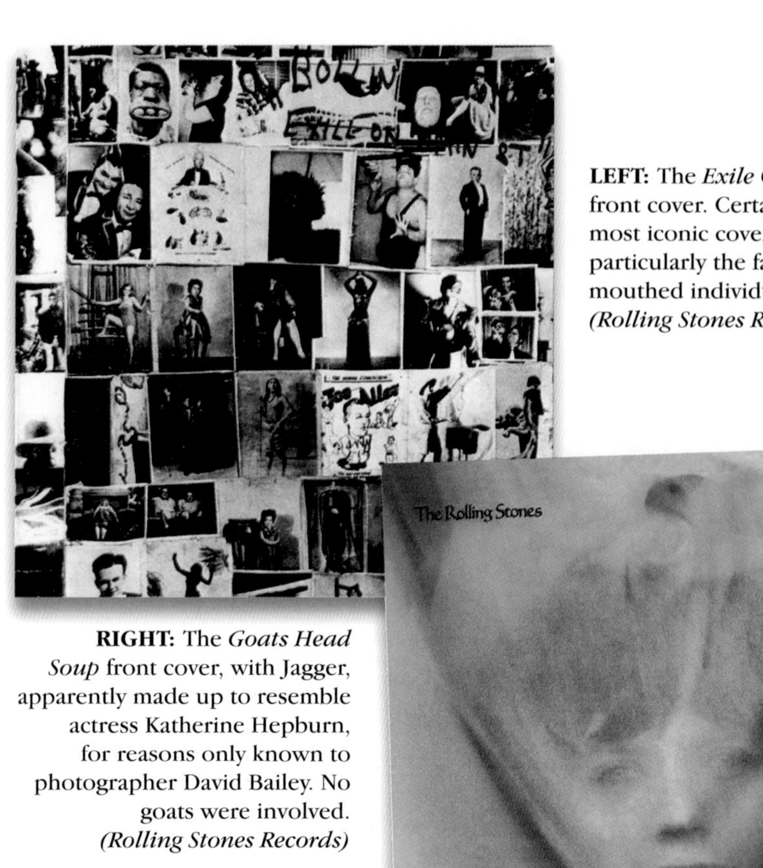

LEFT: The *Exile On Main Street* front cover. Certainly one of the most iconic covers of all time, particularly the famous ball-mouthed individual! *(Rolling Stones Records)*

RIGHT: The *Goats Head Soup* front cover, with Jagger, apparently made up to resemble actress Katherine Hepburn, for reasons only known to photographer David Bailey. No goats were involved. *(Rolling Stones Records)*

LEFT: The *It's Only Rock 'n' Roll* front cover, showing the band either accepting or lampooning their own 'star status,' descending the staircase as heroes. *(Rolling Stones Records)*

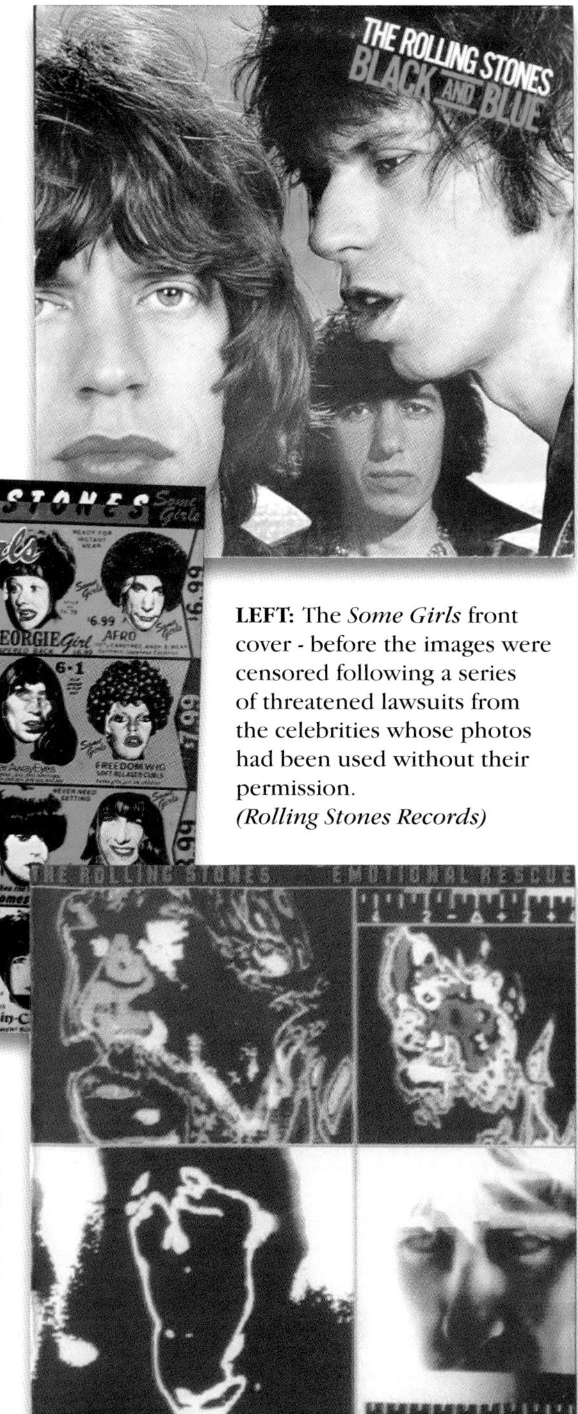

RIGHT: The *Black And Blue* front cover, the first album with Ronnie Wood, though he only played on around half of it. *(Rolling Stones Records)*

LEFT: The *Some Girls* front cover - before the images were censored following a series of threatened lawsuits from the celebrities whose photos had been used without their permission. *(Rolling Stones Records)*

RIGHT: The *Emotional Rescue* front cover. It's an uninspired cover, for what is not a particularly inspired album to usher in the 1980s. *(Rolling Stones Records)*

Left: Keith Richards preshow, with his omnipresent cigarette, at an outdoor late 1970s show. The photo is thought to have been taken by Rita Bedard, who gave it to photographer Curt Angeledes, from whose collection this comes. *(From the collection of Curt Angeledes)*

Above: A rare shot of Keith leaving court in Toronto after his trial for drugs offences in 1978. Very few photos like this exist, as the security guarding Keith as he got into his car and was driven away, was enormous. *(Curt Angeledes)*

Left: Completing a final 'Page of Keef', here is he is onstage in Boulder, Colorado, in 1978, looking effortlessly cool, as ever. It's only rock and roll... but we like it. *(Curt Angeledes)*

to their steadfastly working-class world of getting buses everywhere, getting drunk on Friday nights and, while he is waiting for her, his feet getting wet. She may be, as he describes it, 'a sight for sore eyes', with no money, but still, he waits. In its way, it's a charming little pen-portrait of 1960s working-class Britain, as much so as any Ken Loach film. Dave Mason again appears here, this time on mandolin (though it has been claimed that this was in fact replicated on Mellotron by Nicky Hopkins), while Ric Grech contributes both bowed and plucked violin. Charlie Watts breaks every percussion rule in the book by playing tablas with sticks as opposed to the hands, while the absent Jones is nowhere to be found.

'Salt of the Earth' (Jagger, Richards)

The closing track on the album comes across as something of an anthem for the poor and downtrodden, as Jagger lauds the 'hard-working people', who always get the bad end of the deal. He said in 1970 that the song was 'pure cynicism', saying that the people he sings about have no power, nor ever will, and this makes sense with the lyric. Sure, it is paying its due respect to the 'salt of the earth' people, but nowhere is it espousing any way for them to improve their lot because effectively they are controlled, such that they have no say. The verse about the 'stay at home voter' with his stark 'choice between cancer and polio' hits hard, as it was surely intended to.

Mick and Keith sing this together (Keith takes the first verse, Mick the second, and therewith they do it in harmony). On the third chorus, the Watts Street Gospel Choir from Los Angeles arrives to bolster the song, which again is devoid of Jones. The final minute and a half or so is an instrumental section which picks up the pace a little, in a similar way to 'You Can't Always Get What You Want' from the next album. Leaving aside the Empathy versus Cynicism debate for the moment, it is an infectious and heart-warming song which closes the album brilliantly, in the same way 'Jigsaw Puzzle' did at the end of Side One.

Related Songs:

'Family' (Jagger / Richards)

Recorded during the album sessions, it is a real shame that this track didn't make the cut for the final release as it would have fit perfectly with its largely acoustic style. Jagger's lyric is tremendous, showing a streak of black humour in the tale of a bizarre family and their various dysfunctional lives: father dies in an accident but has his heart replaced by that of the man next door, while his daughter's 'ambition is to be a prostitute, but the breaks just weren't right', and what is worse, she dreams of her father being a client! Meanwhile, the mother is a thrill-seeker who gets sucked into a whirlpool to 'see what the colours of death are all about', and finally the son descends into madness on realising that despite his musical and literary ambitions he has no discernible talent. The song was finally released on the grab-bag compilation

Metamorphosis in 1975.

'Honky Tonk Women' (Jagger, Richards)

The 'trailer single' for the forthcoming *Let It Bleed* album (on which it would surface in an alternative guise as 'Country Honk'), 'Honky Tonk Women' needs no introduction to any music fan who has not been either in a coma or residing on another planet since 1968. Another in the lengthy list of songs which some would argue as 'the definitive Stones single', it was the first record released with Mick Taylor on guitar, having joined the band during the recording of the track in June 1969, at the same time as Brian Jones was being informed that his unreliability (and inability to obtain a US visa for travelling) was resulting in him having to leave the band. Jones died in the swimming pool at his home on 3 July, in circumstances which were shrouded in mystery, conspiracy theory and accusations of foul play for decades to come – 'Honky Tonk Women', the first record without him, was released the very next day, ironically on Independence Day. The following Day, 5 July, the famous Free Concert at Hyde Park dedicated to the memory of Jones took place; this was Taylor's first public appearance with the band.

A 'Honky Tonk Woman' refers, of course, to a woman working (as a dancer, or more) in a Western 'honky-tonk' bar, and Jagger's brilliantly lascivious lyric captures this scenario to perfection. In the first verse, he meets 'a gin-soaked bar-room queen in Memphis', who wants to take him upstairs 'for a ride', but clearly he is drowning his sorrows over another woman as, in the classic verse ending, 'She had to heave me right across her shoulder / 'Cause I just can't seem to drink you off my mind'. Booze-sodden loose raunch 'n roll doesn't come any better than that! There appears to be a reference to cocaine later in the song with the divorcee in New York City who 'blew my nose and then she blew my mind', but Richards claims in his autobiography that this was an example of their way of working that he called 'vowel movement', which involved essentially 'searching for the sounds that work'.

The track opens with the distinctive sound of Jimmy Miller's cowbell – like a whisky glass tapping against someone's teeth – followed by Charlie's drums, and the two are hopelessly out of sync with each other! As Watts has said, the intro was 'an accident', saying that 'either Jimmy was wrong, or I was wrong, but then Keith comes in exactly right, and that makes it work'. Happy accident aside, the intro is so familiar it seems hard to imagine the record without it – although, like 'Jumpin' Jack Flash' before it, the song always starts differently to the record when played live. The verses are sparse, with only the drums and Richards' bluesy guitar licks to accompany Jagger's commanding vocal, but when the chorus comes along, everyone piles in: Wyman with a brilliantly propulsive bassline giving everything a sense of momentum, Nicky Hopkins' piano, horns and female backing vocals (featuring, among others, Doris Troy, who was one of the backing singers on Pink Floyd's *Dark Side of the Moon*). The track was mostly worked out when Taylor came in to overdub guitar, but

Keith credits him with making a big difference, and it's easy to hear why. He comes in just as the song goes into the first chorus, and his strong guitar tone recorded high in the mix, lifts proceedings immediately. He has said that he initially thought he was just doing a session, but that he was so good on the first day that the band knew he was going to be permanent, and that certainly rings true.

The Stones had entered their new phase, one which many believe saw them hit their real stride, in some ways stronger for the departure of the unfortunate Jones. The single hit Number One on both sides of the Atlantic and an incredible run of Stones singles continued apace. It was a run which would continue for quite some time.

Let It Bleed (1969)

Personnel:
Mick Jagger: vocals, harmonica, guitar
Keith Richards: guitar, vocals, bass
Mick Taylor: guitar (two tracks only)
Brian Jones: conga, autoharp (two tracks only)
Bill Wyman: bass, autoharp, vibraphone
Charlie Watts: drums and percussion
With
Nicky Hopkins: piano, organ
Ian Stewart: piano
Ry Cooder: mandolin
Byron Berline: violin
Leon Russell: piano
Bobby Keys: Saxophone
Merry Clayton: vocals
Nanette Workman, Doris Troy, Madeline Bell: backing vocals

Record Label: Decca (UK), London (US)
Recorded: Feb-Nov 1969, produced by Jimmy Miller.
Release Date: December 1969.
Highest chart places: UK: 1, US: 3
Running time: 42:21

Album Facts:

After the release of *Beggars Banquet*, the Stones had occupied themselves with the Rock and Roll Circus vehicle, a bizarre filmed excursion featuring the band playing in a strange circus setting (with Jagger in ringmaster mode), along with guests such as John and Yoko, The Who and Jethro Tull (the latter featuring Tony Iommi during his brief two-week stint with the band). It was immediately shelved and not seen by the public for decades. It was soon time to get back to the serious business of recording again.

Like *Beggars Banquet* before it, *Let It Bleed* contains a mix of lighter songs alongside extremely dark fare. Instrumentally there is much more electric guitar than on the largely acoustic-based *Beggars*, and almost all of these guitars are played by Keith Richards. Brian Jones, in the few recording sessions he attended prior to his June 1969 dismissal, performed only autoharp and vibraphone, on two tracks, while late recruit Mick Taylor only contributed guitar himself to two of the songs (a different two). Thus, the core of the Stones was more or less a quartet this time, and musically massively dependent on Keith, though there is a substantial cast of guest musicians. One of these, singer Nanette Workman, was mistakenly credited on the album as 'Nanette Newman', an actress who had no connection to either her or the band whatsoever!

The majority of the recordings were completed by July 1969 (just a month after Taylor's arrival), with mixing and final overdubs being taken care of in October and December. The finished album was released on 5 December 1969, just one day before the tragic events at the Altamont Speedway show in California, which effectively put the seal on the 'decade of peace and love'. Organising the show (which also included on the bill the Grateful Dead and Jefferson Airplane among others), the band took the misguided advice of the Dead, and enlisted the local Hell's Angels to provide security for the show, paying them with beer. In hindsight, not a decision likely to end well. Throughout the show, violence erupted periodically as the Angels took their Security roles gleefully to heart, wading into unfortunate audience members with pool cues. The Grateful Dead refused to play, seeing the way things were escalating, but the Stones took to the stage as darkness fell. While they were playing 'Under My Thumb' (NOT 'Sympathy for the Devil', as is often claimed), a young black man named Meredith Hunter (who was, for some stupid reason, carrying a hand gun) was stabbed to death right in front of the stage. The Stones played on oblivious to this tragedy until they were made aware by people holding up their hands covered in blood to alert them. That one show crowned Jagger as the Rock and Roll Antichrist, and the Stones as his demonic outriders. The Summer of Love was only two years previously, but as the '70s dawned under this dark pall it may as well have been two decades, or so it seemed to many.

The album title cemented this, of course, and was thought up by Keith Richards. It is often seen as a dark reflection, or corruption, of the Beatles' *Let It Be*, but this album was released a full six months before the Beatles record, and also before the film of the same name. There may have been some link, as Richards has surmised later, as the 'Let It Be' title had been bandied about for the proposed Beatles film for quite some time among those in the know, but to the general public in December 1968 the connection would have been unlikely to have been picked up by many.

Album Cover:

It is well known who was responsible for the bizarre cake adorning the *Let It Bleed* album sleeve, of course – namely a young Delia Smith, darling of the UK 'housewife cookery' shows. The sleeve depicts a vinyl album playing, with the band's name on the label, while above it on the spindle is an assortment of items in place of records, including such layers as a pizza base, a tape or film reel canister (bearing the name of the album on the side), a clock face and, most inexplicably, a bicycle tyre. Atop this 'creation' stands a large and ugly looking cake, with five model figures representing the band (including what looks like Brian Jones). The reverse showed the same tableau in a poorer state of repair: the record is smashed, a slice of pizza sits on it, the album name has been ripped asunder and a slice is cut out of the cake layer. The Stones figures on the top have been destabilised and knocked over. The album title was originally to have been 'Automatic Changer', which explains the record and cake design but does not explain the slightly surprising decision to press on with the design when the final, totally unrelated title was decided upon. Incidentally, Smith claims that her brief was for it to be 'as gaudy as I could make it', which was certainly the case!

Initial copies of the album came with a booklet and an inner sleeve, which contained all of the musician information for each track along with a bold block capital instruction that 'This record should be played loud'.

'Gimme Shelter' (Jagger, Richards)

Just like the previous album, *Let It Bleed* opens with a dark, weighty piece, this time in the shape of the classic 'Gimme Shelter' (it was spelt 'Gimmie' on the album, but subsequent compilations and other versions have corrected this). Written by Keith, the original inspiration for the song took place at his friend Robert Fraser's flat in London, when he was sitting at the window with an acoustic guitar as a tremendous storm hit. He was in something of a dark mood at the time (among other things, Anita Pallenberg was away filming the movie Performance with Jagger at the time, and the proposed nude scene was playing on his mind), and the sight of people running for shelter coalesced in his mind with images of unrest and disaster going on in the world, and the song began to spill out.

The initial sessions for the track were earlier than most of the rest of the album, but the final mixing was not done until November, at which point it was suggested that a female voice might strengthen the track. After an initial invitation to Bonnie Bramlett, one half of the duo Delaney and Bonnie, proved unsuccessful, Jack Nitzsche suggested his friend, American soul and gospel singer Merry Clayton, who would later perform on 'Sweet Home Alabama' by Lynyrd Skynyrd among a host of high-profile sessions. On *Let It Bleed* she is notably miscredited as Mary. Heavily pregnant at the time, and already in bed at the time of the late-night session, she nevertheless came down to the studio immediately and delivered a legendary vocal performance – for once well and truly stealing the thunder from Jagger. If you listen at around the three-minute mark, her voice audibly cracks a couple of times from the power she is imparting, and after the second of these – on the word 'murder', just around three minutes – Jagger's enthused voice can be heard in the background crying 'Woo!' in appreciation. The other significant performance here comes from Richards, whose guitar work is astonishing throughout. The intro, lasting for the first 50 seconds or so of the song, is almost entirely him and has been nominated by many as one of the most hauntingly powerful passages ever recorded.

Tragically, shortly after the session, Clayton suffered a miscarriage, which has often been linked directly to the exertion of her performance – just another example of dark events seemingly following the Stones around like a black dog at the time. Keith has also claimed that just after playing the final note on the final take the neck of his guitar actually fell off, and the song is apocalyptic enough for you to believe it. With Nicky Hopkins joining the Stones quartet on piano again, the track has rarely been surpassed in the band's repertoire, and it went on to provide the title of the film shot of the Altamont show.

'Love in Vain' (Johnson)

Dating from 1937, this Robert Johnson blues lament only came to the attention of Richards and Jagger in 1968, when a second set of vintage Johnson recordings was released, some seven years after the first, *King of the Delta Blues Singers*. While the pair were immediately taken with the song and keen to record it, it is to their credit that they did not attempt to merely recreate Johnson's original, but instead rearranged the song, adding some chords and giving it more of what they would describe as a 'country feel'. It works quite well on the whole and, while it could never exactly be described as the most cheery of songs, it is decidedly less dreary than the original, which really does come across as a Soundtrack for Suicide...

Richards plays some creditable slide guitar on the track – considering he had always left that technique to Jones in the past – while Ry Cooder weighs in with some mandolin pickin'. Cooder was presumably happy enough with this fully credited performance, but he was less content about the sessions as a whole, later bemoaning the fact that the tapes had been left rolling to capture material without his consent for future gain. What he seems to have been referring to there is an album called *Jamming with Edward* which emerged in 1972, featuring a 36-minute jam session featuring Cooder, Hopkins, Wyman, Jagger and Watts (but not the absent Richards who reportedly had major personality issues with Cooder). As if to underline the record's 'official bootleg' status (it did appear on Rolling Stones Records officially), the initial release came with a letter of apology from Jagger for the quality of the album! In truth, while it isn't exactly classic, it's a lot better than its reputation, and Hopkins (who was the 'Edward' of the title via a nickname, also drawing the cover cartoon strip of a man literally laughing his head off) is on particularly great form. Not credited as an official Stones album the record is, nevertheless, worth a listen.

'Country Honk' (Jagger, Richards)

Keith Richards has repeatedly stated that this cheerfully amateur-sounding country romp through 'Honky Tonk Women' represents the way the track was originally planned, but if so, it must be said that we should count our blessings that it was reworked for the infinitely better hit single because this is pretty throwaway stuff. Byron Berline – later to play with The Flying Burrito Brothers, with Gram Parsons who was hanging around with Richards quite a bit at this time – contributes fiddle throughout. Go for the hit version ...

'Live with Me' (Jagger, Richards)

Pure raunch 'n risqué Stones here, with this bizarre yet hilarious appeal by Jagger for the object of his affections to come and live with him, while outlining everything which is wrong with his dysfunctional household: he has 'nasty habits', his best friend 'shoots water rats and feeds them to his geese' (a rare example of the word 'geese' in rock and roll wordplay there), he has 'harebrained children locked in the nursery' who have 'earphone heads, they got dirty necks, they're so 20th century'. He must have plentiful resources, as he has servants, but even then the cook is a 'whore' who gets together with the butler 'behind the pantry door', while the French maid is 'wild for Crazy Horse', strips for the chauffeur and causes 'the footman's eyes to get crossed'. Marvellous stuff!

Musically this is equally good. This was the first track Mick Taylor played on (his only other appearance on the album is 'Country Honk'), and he trades licks superbly with Richards, foreshadowing their dual guitar trademark, which Richards would term 'weaving', after the way they would weave in and out of each other, alternating rhythm and lead playing. Also making a first appearance on this track is saxophonist Bobby Keys, who was to make a number of appearances on Stones records over the next few years. Hopkins is again present and on good form, while Leon Russell makes his only appearance on a Stones track supplying piano and a horn arrangement. Wyman does not appear on this track as Richards, who was developing an instinctive knack for a great bassline, handles the bass here and does so magnificently and imaginatively.

'Let It Bleed' (Jagger, Richards)

A simple, no-nonsense, lyrically suggestive blues track – no more, no less – with the euphemisms for sex and drugs becoming so glaring as to threaten to leave behind the art of the double entendre and simply head straight for the lowest common denominator and settle for 'single entendres'! The reference to 'there'll always be space for you in my parking spot' allegedly refers to the fact that her 'parking lot' was how Marianne Faithful described her 'feminine area', shall we say! Musically it fits the lyrical content, with a loose, sloppy sound heavily featuring Ian Stewart's bouncy piano (the only track on the album he played on). Overall, it's fun for a while, but as it approaches the five-and-a-half minute mark it does begin to seriously overstay its welcome. Not a highlight.

'Midnight Rambler' (Jagger, Richards)

A lengthy, ominous seven-minute Chicago blues excursion which takes its lyrical inspiration directly from the courtroom testimony of Albert DeSalvo, who confessed to being the notorious 'Boston Strangler' in 1964. The song casts Jagger in the role of the late-night stalker, and he clearly relishes it. Beginning at a mid-paced tempo, the song speeds up across the first couple of verses until it breaks down to almost nothing after an almost ambient mid-section which sees Jagger repeating 'Don't do that' seemingly endlessly before the music crumples in on itself and restarts at a slow pace again, only to rebuild toward the climax. In truth, the track does drag a little across its length, but it would come into its own far more as a live showcase, whereupon Jagger would employ menacing theatrics, often crawling across the stage, lashing the floor with his belt, under subdued and sombre lighting.

Jagger contributes harmonica throughout the song, with Jones, rather sadly, credited with effectively inaudible percussion. He is supposed to have played congas on the track, but there is little evidence of it. It may have been a final 'gift' of a credit if his part was mixed out of the final track. Oddly enough, this supremely dark, violent piece was written by Jagger and Richards during a short break in the idyllic surroundings of the Italian village of Positano. As Jagger himself commented in an interview with Rolling Stone some 25 years later, 'Why we should write such a dark song in this beautiful, sunny place, I really don't know. We wrote everything there – the tempo changes, everything. And I'm playing the harmonica in these little cafes, and there's Keith with the guitar...'

'You Got the Silver' (Jagger, Richards)

The first ever solo lead vocal from Keith Richards for an entire song, this is a track which was written by him pretty much entirely. A simple lyrical expression of love towards a third party, widely thought to be Anita Pallenberg, its sub-three minute duration is fitting for what is, essentially, a pleasantly Dylan-esque country song (one could imagine it fitting onto *Nashville Skyline* quite easily). It threatens to be a little dull until the drums enter toward the end and give things a welcome, quite bouncy, lease of life. There was an alternative version recorded, with Jagger singing, but Keith's performance got the nod on this occasion. The hapless Jones gets his only other credit of the album here, for playing autoharp, but this is rather hard to make out on the original release (it is, conversely, mixed much higher and is far more audible on the unreleased (but bootlegged) Jagger rendition). Hopkins is very prominent here with some commendable piano and organ, and there is an uncredited slide guitar part from Ry Cooder.

Interestingly, Keith only got the chance to do the vocal in the first place through an engineering error. Glyn Johns had been asked by producer Jimmy Miller to apply some backward reverb to a guitar part on the song, and while doing so he accidentally deleted Jagger's vocal! The singer was in Australia at the time, working on the film Ned Kelly, so Keith was asked to step up to the plate – and even when Jagger was able to redo his part, the Richards vocal was preferred.

'Monkey Man' (Jagger, Richards)

Another song written by Jagger and Richards during their stay in Positano, on the Italian Amalfi coast, this is a puzzling one lyrically. It has been claimed to have been written in tribute to the Italian pop artist Mario Schifano but, although the pair did meet the artist on a film set around that time, self-references to their own past with lines such as 'I hope we're not too messianic, or a trifle too satanic, we love to play the blues' suggest a meaning closer to home. Many interpretations, from the fairly prosaic (recounting a drug experience), through the sociological (examining and satirising their own relationship with the press and the media) and all the way to the outlandish (a reference to good versus evil, using the monkey metaphor to highlight Satan sometimes being described as 'the monkey of god'). Whatever the truth of it, it's a nice pop/rock sort of song, with particular praise being reserved for Nicky Hopkins' tremendous piano in the introduction, reminiscent of the Doors' 'Riders on the Storm' which would, of course, not appear for over a year. Bill Wyman plays the vibraphone on this track.

'You Can't Always Get What You Want' (Jagger, Richards)

The true 'epic' of the album, and one which has remained a live favourite until the present day, this is a track with a great number of twists and turns throughout its seven-and-a-half-minute duration. The most startling is the opening, whereby the first minute or so is occupied by the London Bach Choir singing the chorus unaccompanied, following which a short French horn part enters, just before Jagger begins the first verse. In truth, that opening section with the rather stilted, wooden delivery of the choir could easily have been dispensed with, and arguably would have made the track the stronger for it. Still, plenty of people seem to like it, so it is what it is.

Once we get past that bit of choral 'fluff', the song proper starts with Jagger almost unaccompanied, but over the course of the track, the instrumentation builds and builds until, towards the end, a quite thrilling tempo change leads us to a breathless conclusion. It is notable that Charlie Watts doesn't play on this track – he was having trouble getting the 'feel' right, and Jimmy Miller (a drummer himself) showed him what he envisioned. So impressive was Miller's take that they elected to leave it as it was, so it is indeed Jimmy Miller that you hear on drums. Al Kooper – famous from Dylan's 'Like A Rolling Stone' among many others – contributes organ and piano (and that little French horn bit, incidentally), while Rocky Dijon is back with additional percussion. Kooper actually did a full score for horns, but in the end, the band ignored all of it except his French horn cameo! Doris Troy, Madeline Bell and Nanette Workman all chime in with backing vocals, and do a sterling job. The choir are uncredited – this is because they asked their name to be removed after hearing the lyrics to 'Live with Me', which seems somewhat of an over-reaction. Allegedly, Jagger responded that they should be happy enough because Christopher Marlowe's poem 'The Passionate Shepherd to His Love' begins with the similarly phrased 'Come live with me and be my love', which met with something of a stony reception!

There are some interesting characters in the lyrics – the girl at the reception is widely thought to be Marianne Faithfull, while the part about going down to the demonstration probably harks back to the 1968 demo that Jagger attended and got inspiration for 'Street Fighting Man'. The most widely debated, however, is 'Mr Jimmy', whom Jagger meets in the 'Chelsea drugstore' and goes for the 'cherry red' soda with. Many have claimed this to be a reference either to Jimmy Miller or even Jimi Hendrix, who was living in London at the time. The most often accepted wisdom, however, is that the drugstore in question was in Excelsior, Minnesota (with Chelsea being substituted in the lyrics in order to scan) and that Mr Jimmy was a well-known local character called Jimmy Hutmaker, who always went by the name Mr Jimmy, according to locals. There is anecdotal evidence that Jagger did meet him, and there is even a story that Jimmy ordered a cherry coke while with Jagger, only to be served with a regular one, to which he responded 'You can't always have what you want' – but Mick has never confirmed or denied this.

Related Songs:

'Memo from Turner' (Jagger, Richards)

Featured on the soundtrack of the movie Performance, and credited to Mick Jagger rather than the Stones when released as a single, Jagger is indeed the only Stone to appear on this aggressive, Dylan-esque bluesy rocker with a snarling vocal performance setting it apart. Jagger desperately wanted Richards to appear on it, and indeed put it forward for inclusion on *Let It Bleed*, but Keith, harbouring a grudge possibly not unrelated to Jagger's appearance with Anita Pallenberg in the film, flatly refused on both counts. There were, in fact, three versions recorded: the first featured Steve Winwood and Jim Capaldi from Traffic among others, the second actually did involve Richards, and possibly Bill Wyman also, while the third, and officially released version, took the vocal from the first recording and put it to a new backing featuring the dominant slide guitar of Ry Cooder, along with Russ Titelman (guitar), Jerry Scheff (bass), Randy Newman (organ) and Gene Parsons (drums). The second recording eventually surfaced on the compilation album Metamorphosis in 1975. The B-side of the single was a somewhat inconsequential instrumental entitled 'Natural Magic', written by Jack Nitzsche and lasting just over a minute and a half. Jagger allegedly contributes maracas.

'Downtown Suzie' (Wyman)

This is a light and an inconsequential piece which eventually turned up on the grab-bag *Metamorphosis*, and this 'trying to be funny but failing' nugget is the only other Stones song to fall from the pen of Bill Wyman, after 'In Another Land'. The music is alternately happy and brash and painfully 'novelty' in style, and drags hopelessly in places. If you ever wondered why Wyman did not write more songs for the band, simply listen to this. It has Ry Cooder on slide, but not a whole lot else.

'Jiving Sister Fanny' (Jagger, Richards)

Recorded during the *Let It Bleed* sessions but never totally finished (the lyrics were apparently largely made up on the spot, and it shows), the song shows some promise but no more. The lurching riff had the makings of a good song in it, while the guitar solo (by either Richards or Taylor – it is unconfirmed) is good but much too high in the mix, the vocal melody meanders and goes nowhere and the whole thing is something of a mess. Once again, this showed up on the half-cooked semi-disaster which was the unauthorised *Metamorphosis* compilation.

Sticky Fingers (1971)

Personnel:
Mick Jagger: vocals, guitar, percussion
Keith Richards: guitar, vocals
Mick Taylor: guitar
Bill Wyman: bass, piano
Charlie Watts: drums and percussion
With
Nicky Hopkins: piano, organ
Ian Stewart: piano
Ry Cooder: guitar
Rocky Dijon: congas
Billy Preston: organ
Bobby Keys: Saxophone
Jim Dickinson: piano
Jack Nitzsche: piano
Jim Price: trumpet, piano

Record Label: Rolling Stones Records
Recorded: December 1969-October 1970, produced by Jimmy Miller.
Release Date: April 1971.
Highest chart places: UK: 1, US: 1
Running time: 46:25

Album Facts:

After things had been getting increasingly strained between the Stones and Decca/London Records, something had to give. This came in the form of the band following the Beatles' 'Apple' lead and setting up their own record label, Rolling Stones Records. Featuring the distinctive yellow label with the iconic 'tongue and lips' logo, the label released a handful of albums by other artists, but by comparison with other 'vanity labels' such as Apple, Purple Records or Led Zeppelin's Swan Song made very little effort to sign outside artists to the roster, mainly concentrating on Stones-related releases. The first album released on the label was *Sticky Fingers* in 1971, and what a milestone album it proved to be.

Some of the material which eventually ended up on the album had been floating around since the *Let It Bleed* sessions (indeed, it is claimed that *Sticky Fingers* was actually an early working title for the *Let It Bleed* album), but most of the material was recorded at sessions during 1971 – once again, spread out over a period of months rather than in one large chunk of studio time. Again, there was a host of guest artists – including no less than four piano players as well as Billy Preston on organ, which does beg the question as to why the band never featured a full-time keyboard member, after Ian Stewart was dropped for being too old (or too ugly, depending whose version you believe)! Continuing along the same 'rock and roll band with country and blues elements' as the previous record, it refined and refocused that approach, resulting in what many see as the band's best album to this point. Certainly, they were by now firmly ensconced in a remarkable run of albums which would not falter until the mid-'70s.

The split from Decca Records became more ill-tempered after the label demanded the band honour their outstanding commitments by delivering one more studio recording for a single. The band duly did this, by the letter of the law, but the track in question was never going to get a release, that much is certain. It's title? 'Cocksucker Blues'! A sparse blues, featuring Jagger accompanied by a simple acoustic guitar backing relating a disturbing tale of a schoolboy drawn to London only to drift into a life of homosexual prostitution and occurrences of abuse at the hands of the police, it is a powerful piece in its own right, but has never seen an official release to this day. There was a brisk trade in bootleg vinyl single pressings back in the day, but Decca quietly consigned it to the vaults. Plainly stung by this, they put out a UK compilation of old Stones tracks including some which had only appeared on US releases at the time, and rather provocatively released it on the same day as *Sticky Fingers*! Titled *Stone Age*, it prompted the band to take out a full-page advertisement in the UK music press disowning the album and urging fans against buying it. What appears to have been the chief irritant in this whole episode was the sleeve design, which consisted of the title and band members' names written in graffiti on a wall, in what was clearly a reference to the very sleeve design they had so publicly rejected for *Beggars Banquet*. One can understand the reaction of the band on seeing this! A string of unauthorised and often sub-par compilations would continue emanating from the Decca archives throughout the next few years.

Album Cover:

There can be few people with half an interest in rock music who are unaware of this, one of the most iconic sleeve designs ever to be released. Its fame - or infamy - rested on one single element: the zip fastener. Conceived by legendary pop-artist Andy Warhol and then designed by Craig Braun, the front cover shows the crotch of a man in a pair of blue jeans (the back cover shows the rear view), with an actual working zip for the fly. On opening the zip - and also the cardboard mock-belt buckle above - the same crotch is visible inside, clad in a pair of distinctly unflattering white underpants, which have the name of Andy Warhol written on them. The model for these shots was apparently Glenn O'Brien, who was editor of Warhol's magazine Interview, though several different men were photographed before the final shots were selected. There is also a card insert sheet with a black and white photo of the band happily messing around for the camera, while the other side has a large red image of the celebrated tongue logo (here for the first time, designed by John Pasche), together with the album credits. Beyond its award-winning originality of design and artistic statement of intent, the sleeve resulted in somewhat more practical issues: initial shipments of the album had to be withdrawn as the zip was causing damage to the album (specifically the track 'Sister Morphine'), so subsequent stock was shipped with the zip pulled down so that it would only impact the label. This didn't save the record collections of millions of fans, however (including the author!), who saw the albums with the misfortune of being next before this one in their racks having their sleeves damaged by the zip! If this was you, you'd remember it...

In Spain the relatively stringent Franco regime banned the sleeve immediately (along with 'Sister Morphine', which they replaced with 'Let It Rock'). Instead, they substituted it with a bizarre design (by Pasche, along with Phil Jude) which showed an opened can of treacle with – literally – sticky fingers emerging from it. So – zip, no, but disembodied fingers, why certainly! Once again, this was hard to fathom censorship.

'Brown Sugar' (Jagger, Richards)

Released as a single the week before the album, 'Brown Sugar' continues the run of classic Stones singles, rivalling even 'Jumpin' Jack Flash' or 'Satisfaction' for the title of 'definitive Stones 45'. This time around the song was almost all Jagger's work. He wrote most of the words and music while on a break from filming Ned Kelly in Australia, coming up with the famous riff on electric guitar. Even Richards nods to this, as he admits that, though he considers himself 'the riff master', this song was one where Jagger got the better of him. Of course, he got to put his own stamp on it when he played it, in open tuning on a five-string guitar – a Richards trademark by this time – in a fashion which sounded like no-one else. There are strong contributions on piano and sax from Ian Stewart and Bobby Keys; in fact, the instrumental section mid-song was originally designated for a Mick Taylor guitar solo, but when Keys played his sax part it was immediately edited into the song at the expense of Taylor's part. It is now difficult to imagine the track without it. In some ways this was where the Stones signature 'recipe' of being loose and raw without being sloppy really came to full fruition, as evidenced by the backing vocals being recorded by Mick and Keith, standing at the same microphone and passing a bottle of bourbon between them! There can be no doubt that the earthiness and urgency of this approach can clearly be heard, and makes the track come alive.

The lyrics to the track were contentious to say the least, with Jagger bringing in such topics as abuse of slaves, oral and interracial sex and also drugs, as the 'brown sugar' of the title, of course, refers to heroin, as well as the (no doubt intentionally portrayed) equally 'addictive' female subjects of the song. Jagger himself later admitted that he had 'no idea what I was going on about' in the song, getting in 'all the nasty subjects in one go'. He also stated that he would not write a song such as that in later years, as he would 'probably censor myself' – and indeed he would go on to do just that very often in live performances of the song, replacing the line 'hear him whip the women just around midnight' with the alternative 'you should have heard him just around midnight. At the time, however, in 1971, the idea of the Stones shying away from anything controversial or offensive would have been the last thing on anyone's mind. They were everyone's favourite bête noire, for good or otherwise!

'Sway' (Jagger, Richards)

This one is Jagger's song all the way. Keith had very little involvement in it at all – in fact, he doesn't even play on the track, apart from contributing some backing vocals. The reason for this isn't any sort of refusal to play on it – it is simply that the recording was done at Mick's Stargroves house, which Richards hated travelling down to, and he was simply absent at the time. As a result, Jagger provides the rhythm guitar part (nicely distorted, in open tuning) in his first electric guitar part on a Stones song. His bleak, somewhat enigmatic lyric has also been something of a talking point over the years. Sounding remarkably like Van Morrison, especially in the opening verse, the way he mangles the words at times has led to many conflicting misheard lyrics. In particular, while the chorus line is universally published as 'It's just that demon life has got me in its sway', many have heard it as 'evil eye' or 'forgot me in its sway'. Whatever the truth of this, what is certain is that it is one of the few rock songs to quote the philosophical notion of 'circular time', as debated by such luminaries as Frederick Nietzsche! The first verse has our reluctant hero awakening to a day which is presumably so bad that it has 'destroyed' his 'notion of circular time'. Well, we've all thought that I suppose.

While the lyric once again illustrates Jagger's literate, well-read and articulate style as a wordsmith of underrated worth, the track also gives Mick Taylor his first real turn in the Stones spotlight, as he contributes two excellent solos – the first being with the bottleneck slide and the extended closing one without. Nicky Hopkins contributes the piano part here, while Paul Buckmaster (who worked on other key 1970s tracks as Bowie's 'Space Oddity' and Elton John's 'Your Song') did the string arrangement, albeit with the strings mixed quite low. Pete Townshend and Ronnie Lane have been reported as contributing backing vocals, but this is not definitively confirmed. An unfairly overlooked track, it probably suffered for coming up immediately after 'Brown Sugar', a hard act to follow in anyone's book.

'Wild Horses' (Jagger, Richards)

The Stones show their Country side again here for this beautifully affecting ballad, and they absolutely knock it out of the park. Originally conceived and part-written by Keith as an expression of how hard it was leaving his new son Marlon and going away on tour, the words were later largely rewritten by Jagger to astonishing effect. The song can be seen as having many meanings, from a simple love song, to others such as a man who is dying, a couple who never quite get their relationship to work until they get older and their time is short, or even the less romantic idea of drug addiction. Whatever the actual truth behind it, the genius of the song is that it can be equally powerful in different ways depending on the person who is hearing it. It has certainly been played many, many time at funerals, capturing the moment to heart-breaking perfection, and there must certainly have been a great number of people who have felt a line such as 'I have my freedom, but I don't have much time' hit them like a punch in the gut, for different personal reasons. 'Wild Horses' is full of moments like that, and the way Mick gets inside the song emotionally marks it out as one of his greatest performances, showing just how good a singer he actually always has been.

It has often been claimed to have been written about Marianne Faithfull, but in the liner notes to the 1993 compilation *Jump Back,* Jagger claims that this was not the case, as he is sure the timeline didn't fit with their break-up. For her part, Faithfull has claimed that 'Wild Horses couldn't drag me away' was the first thing she said to Mick after she awoke from a six-day coma following a sleeping pill overdose in 1969, but even if so, this probably did not inspire the use of the phrase as originally written by Richards. Keith plays the lead lines on this, brilliantly dovetailing with Jagger's voice with a stunning feel for the spirit of country balladry. Mick Taylor plays some superbly supportive acoustic guitar, while the piano part is contributed by a session player named Jim Dickinson, who just happened to be in the studio that day. Ian Stewart, who was originally going to play, threw an astonishing tantrum upon seeing that the song, quite reasonably given its nature, contained a lot of minor chords. Bizarrely describing such chords as 'Chinese music' before storming off in a ridiculous fashion, Dickinson offered his services and was such forever associated with a classic.

The country feel of the song comes from the time it was first worked on by Keith – as long ago as 1969 – when he was spending a lot of time with country-rock pioneer Gram Parsons, who had steered the Byrds down that road in such a successful manner. Influenced by Parsons, in the same way as Parsons was influenced by the Stones, his feel for the music really shone through. Parsons in fact recorded the song a year before the Stones version was released, with his own band The Flying Burrito Brothers on their 1970 album *Burrito Delux*e. The Stones version was released as a single in America and other territories (with 'Sway' on the flip), but strangely not in the UK, where one feels it would have surely been very successful, appealing even to an audience far from the hardcore Stones crowd. Perhaps they felt the public was not ready for a Stones single which was an unashamed ballad – something which would be very much remedied later in the decade with 'Angie' and 'Fool to Cry'.

'Can't You Hear Me Knocking' (Jagger, Richards)

A totally different ballpark again for this seven-minute-plus part song/part jam. The opening three minutes or so see the band delivering a low-down, dirty garage-rock track with no airs and graces and no frills. The lyrics are interesting ('plastic boots', 'satin shoes' and 'cocaine eyes'), but really they are simply there to sound good against the choppy, staccato guitar-riffing backdrop. At just over two-and-a-half minutes things drop back to just Rocky Dijon's congas before the band ease their way back in. Bobby Keys starts playing a totally improvised saxophone solo which builds in a nice jazzy way over almost two minutes before Mick Taylor comes in and takes over from around four-and-a-half minutes in with a beautifully smooth guitar solo, reminiscent of Carlos Santana, to take the song past the seven-minute mark. During this, the Latin feel seems to increase with the percussion of Dijon and Jimmy Miller joined by Billy Preston with a great, fat organ sound, and the final minute or so has the whole ensemble locked into a tremendous groove. This was the Stones really stretching out in a comfortable and confident manner and remains enormously popular.

According to both Taylor and Richards, the whole second half of the track – the 'jam' section – was something totally off-the-cuff and not even planned to happen. Taylor says that he just felt like playing on, and the others picked up their instruments again and joined in, while Richards recalls that they didn't even realise the tape was still rolling until they heard the playback. From such happy accidents are rock classics sometimes born.

'You Gotta Move' (McDowell)

A traditional gospel blues song with numerous recorded versions dating back to the 1940s, the song was brought back into the public eye somewhat in the early 1960s when Gary Davis (1962) and Mississippi Fred McDowell (1964) produced their versions. The Stones took their own recording straight from the McDowell 'Delta Blues' version and indeed gave credit to him as songwriter – which, while not strictly true, did acknowledge their debt to his arrangement, and also helped him to a comfortable life before he passed away not too long afterwards, in 1972. Some vinyl pressings of *Sticky Fingers* credited McDowell on the label, while others bore no writing credit, but it appears that he did receive royalties.

Musically, there is not too much of significance to say about the track, barring the aforementioned McDowell arrangement. Jagger delivers the song in an overly affected Southern US dialect accompanied by Taylor's slide guitar, and overall it veers dangerously close to parody. The band had been playing the song regularly on their 1969 world tour, but there doesn't seem too much justification behind treating it to this sparse studio rendition.

'Bitch' (Jagger, Richards)

Side Two of the vinyl opens with the Stones once again finding themselves in trouble with the censors, with this snappy, hotwired rocker which also saw active service as the B-side to 'Brown Sugar', along with a serviceable live version of Chuck Berry's 'Let It Rock' (itself a clone of 'Johnny B Goode'). When various radio station personnel took a look at the title, the shutters went down immediately, and the track was banned from airplay at the time across a host of different stations. It is true that the song is fairly sexual in nature, but not offensively so – and it appears that the title word was the cause of the uproar. Mick Jagger himself attempted to ease this tension by pointing out that the chorus referred to 'love' being a bitch, and that this was the only use of the word, but of course, this cut no ice. Who was going to listen to Mick Jagger's reassurances about their outrage in 1971 anyway?

The track itself is a cracker. Opening with Richards' aggressive buzzsaw riff, it never lets up the pace or energy throughout its three-and-a-half minutes. In actual fact, the song was mostly down to Jagger, but according to engineer Andy Johns, Keith had a typically crucial role in developing the track. The session was again at Stargroves, and Keith had arrived much later than the others, and the rest of the band (plus Bobby Keys) were working on the song, which simply wasn't working. Johns remembers coming out of the kitchen and seeing Richards sitting on the floor, barefoot, eating a bowl of cereal. Apparently, he suddenly said 'hand me that guitar', strapped the instrument on and immediately kicked the song's tempo up and transformed it there and then from a rather sluggishly dull affair to its final form. As Johns said, he just thought to himself 'Ah, THAT'S what he does!'

The band are helped out on the track by a horn section of Bobby Keys and Jim Price (the latter on trumpet), who double up the riff as well as embellishing other parts of the song. They certainly add some muscle and give the riff a very distinctive power, but some have still remained of the opinion that the track would be better left to the guitar to carry it. Very much a matter of taste. It is Richards, incidentally, who contributes the lengthy solo towards the end of the track, as well as the lead licks throughout, showing that however good Taylor was turning out to be, he himself was still no slouch.

'I Got the Blues' (Jagger, Richards)

Southern blues and soul this time out, as Jagger overlays the languid backing with a despairing tale of a man who has been abandoned by his lover and, cheerfully, contemplates suicide with the happy line 'I'll bust my brains out for you'. Well, thanks Mick, but I've just had the carpets cleaned...

It would appear that he isn't blameless in this situation, as he does find himself hoping at one point that she finds herself a man who 'won't drag you down with abuse'. It is strongly considered to be in direct reference to Jagger's break-up with Marianne Faithfull, but again this isn't conclusive. The horns of Keys and Price are again strongly featured, and there is an excellent organ solo courtesy of Billy Preston which raises the track on its own, but overall it is a lesser number on the album and something of a dirge.

'Sister Morphine' (Jagger, Richards, Faithfull)

A rare credit for someone in addition to Jagger and Richards, in this case, Marianne Faithfull who wrote some of the lyrics (how much is open to argument, and indeed has been argued between the parties concerned). There was no credit for her on the original release of the album, but after a lawsuit, this was rectified with CD reissues a couple of decades later. Indeed, Faithfull released her own version of the song as a single a couple of years earlier in 1969 (with accompaniment from Jagger and Watts), but while she was credited as co-writer on the UK Decca release, the US London Records single omitted her, which only added to the confusion. She recorded the song again in the late 1970s.

The song itself, according to Faithfull, concerns a man who is in hospital badly injured following an accident and asking for morphine to take away his pain, knowing that he will probably soon die from his injuries and that 'this shot will be my last'. Others have claimed that he is more likely an addict receiving treatment but wanting to score desperately, and possibly overdosing in the end. There are lines which are up for interpretation, such as his wondering 'why does the doctor have no face' and also the claim that 'things are not as they seem'. Whatever the actual intent of the lyric, it is a harrowing and desolate piece, with Jagger's anguished vocal accompanied by the regular band (apart from Taylor, who does not play on this) together with Ry Cooder on slide guitar and Jack Nietzsche on very creepy sounding piano. It is difficult not to be affected by the final, despairing 'You know and I know, in the morning I'll be dead / And you can sit around, and you can watch, all the clean white sheets stained red'. The Stones never ever got darker than this.

'Dead Flowers' (Jagger, Richards)

In which we see the old trick of following something dark with something cheerful by way of contrast. Or do we? In actual fact, from a lyrical standpoint, we certainly do not as this straight country tune tells of the breakdown in relations between Jagger's down-on-his-luck character and a woman who seems to be living the high life in satin chairs and Cadillacs. In fact, while she is in her 'rose-pink Cadillac', he is to be found 'in my basement room with a needle and a spoon'. The chorus has him telling her she can 'send me dead flowers to my wedding, and I won't forget to put roses on your grave'.

The kicker with this track is that the music accompanying these lyrics is unflinchingly upbeat and bouncy. Jagger delivers the song in a full-on Country-and-Western accent so broad he may as well be wearing cowboy boots and a ten-gallon hat, and the lyrics do take on a little sense of black humour owing to this. It's a slightly disconcerting yet brilliantly effective juxtaposition of moods, and – Jagger's over-the-top delivery notwithstanding – it manages to be more of a genuinely great country song than a mere parody. It is clear that the music is not mournful in any case, as the piano is provided by Ian 'No Minor Chords' Stewart himself, who gambols along quite lustily in accompaniment.

'Moonlight Mile' (Jagger, Richards)

The closing song on the album is quite different to anything the Stones had done up to this point, being a wistful, almost jazzy, ballad about life on the road accompanied by meandering string sections which take the mind lazily off to nostalgic avenues given the slightest excuse. Another song which is almost entirely a Jagger composition (with some input from Taylor), Keith Richards didn't even turn up for the session, making this the first song in the band's history that he takes no part in whatsoever. Still gets a writing credit though!

Jagger has said that the idea first came to him during a late-night train journey far from home, and certainly, the lyrics conjure up the loneliness and boredom suffered by someone on a long journey by either train or tour bus, far from his loved ones. He de-glamourises the rock star life by making 'a rag pile of my shiny clothes', just to keep out the cold, and he wistfully recounts how there is not even a radio signal to keep him company. He yearns for his lover's company, but he is 'just about a moonlight mile down the road'. Jim Price abandons his usual trumpet to provide a superbly effective piano part, while the string score by Paul Buckmaster takes things to another level entirely. The final section of the song is almost ambient in feel, as the piano and strings seem to be calling to each other in as lonely a manner as the protagonist. Unexpected, subtle, understated and quite beautiful, it is the perfect way to close what is unquestionably the strongest Stones album up to this point – and which many would argue as their strongest ever.

Related Song:

'Travelin' Man' (Jagger, Richards)

Recorded during the album sessions but never used, this track is basically a vehicle for Mick Taylor, who handles all of the guitar work on a rough yet exciting track which is clearly part-jam. Taylor solos away massively high in the mix throughout this six-minute-plus out-take which is manna from heaven for admirers of the mercurially talented guitarist, of whom there are many. It's clearly unfinished and needs a severe polishing, but this is a complete blast of enthusiastic balls-out rocking by a band clearly having a whale of a time.

Exile on Main Street (1972)

Personnel:
Mick Jagger: vocals, guitar, percussion, harmonica
Keith Richards: guitar, vocals, bass, piano
Mick Taylor: guitar, bass
Bill Wyman: bass
Charlie Watts: drums and percussion
With
Nicky Hopkins: piano, organ
Ian Stewart: piano
Bill Plummer: double bass
Al Perkins: pedal steel guitar
Billy Preston: organ
Bobby Keys: Saxophone
Jack Nitzsche: piano
Jim Price: trumpet
Jimmy Miller: drums
Clydie King, Venetta Fields, Joe Green: backing vocals

Record Label: Rolling Stones Records
Recorded: June 1971-March 1972, produced by Jimmy Miller.
Release Date: May 1972.
Highest chart places: UK: 1, US: 1
Running time: 67:07

Album Facts:

This landmark double album saw the band literally in the position of exiles, having left the UK in the spring of 1971 for tax reasons (their tax arrears were apparently so substantial that they could not afford to pay them back). Richards had moved to a sprawling house called Nellcôte, just outside Nice in the South of France, and the album was recorded in the basement there using the band's mobile recording studio (which they had begun using in the same way at Stargroves during the *Sticky Fingers* sessions. The album famously has a loose, sloppy feel to it, whereby the experience of the whole is more satisfying than listening to individual tracks because the listener grows accustomed to the sound. This was largely due to the sessions for the album, which were anything but disciplined, taking place from about 8 pm to 3 am each night, and including whatever other musicians and assorted hangers-on were staying there at the time – Richards was in the grip of his heroin habit by this time, along with Pallenberg, and the couple did not exactly run a tight ship when it came to controlling their guests. As a result, Wyman and Watts are absent on some tracks as neither of them were substance users of any kind, and Wyman, in particular, hated the whole atmosphere and ambience of the sessions. Jagger also kept his distance from the more 'social' aspects, as he was already by this time quite focused on keeping in shape both for his voice and his onstage energy levels. Richards, Taylor, Keys, Jimmy Miller and Andy Johns, on the other hand, partied enthusiastically, with Miller's indulgence especially leading to problems on the production side – Jagger claimed later that he himself had to salvage some of the mixes, and that he was very dissatisfied with much of the production.

Album Cover:

The album cover was designed by John Van Hamersveld, but the initial idea came from Jagger. One day, with Watts, he had been browsing bookshops and come upon some photographs by 1950s 'Beat' photographer Robert Frank, in particular, a book called The Americans, which featured a series of photos from across the US States, during a road trip. Some of the key photos later used on the front cover, featuring circus sideshow performers, came from this book. Among them was perhaps the most famous image – the strange guy with three balls in his mouth. This was, in fact, a 1930s performer known as 'Three Ball Charlie', and the balls were in fact, amazing as it may seem, a tennis ball, a golf ball and a billiard ball! The 'Joe Allen' featured in a poster-style picture was a contortionist from the same period. Frank, who was still a working photographer, also took some photos of the Stones (mainly Jagger in fact) on Main Street itself in Los Angeles for the cover, which were largely used on the back cover. The inside spread features more photos of Jagger, some handwritten notes by him and, somewhat randomly, a screaming Joan Crawford. The inner sleeves had photos which were monochrome again but in this case red/white and green/white respectively, and also the song credits. Finally, there was a perforated strip of twelve postcards, which originated from a band shoot by Norman Seeffe which had smoke, confetti and all manner of things prepared. Keith arrived very late for the shoot, in less than pristine condition, and as soon as the camera rolled, he proceeded to fall about all over the set. It was a one-off set-up, so there would be no repeat shoot, but Richards himself suggested using the images (which were deemed unusable for the cover) as postcards, and so they were.

'Rocks Off' (Jagger, Richards)

This opening track is a perfect salvo to announce the coming album. It's murky, it's loose, it's haphazardly mixed – but it contains pure Stones magic. Recorded during one of the sweltering nights in the Nellcôte basement, engineer Andy Johns was led a merry dance by Richards who, after a lot of work on the song earlier, kept falling asleep during the recording sessions. The intercom wasn't working and, tired of having to walk out of the control room each time to wake him up, Johns simply left the tape running. When all was done, Keith made his way to the control room to hear the playback of what they'd captured – and promptly fell asleep again immediately! As this was now about 3 am, Johns assumed the session was over for the night and left to drive back the 40 minutes to the villa where he was staying. As soon as he arrived there he received a phone call from an irritated Richards asking why he had left, as he had just had an idea for another guitar part. Back in the car, back to the studio he went. However, as he said later, the part that Keith had come up with, involving two rhythm guitar parts, one in each side of the stereo mix, was so good that he was glad to be called back.

Jagger's lyrics for this one are quite obscure, but a certain amount of the imagery certainly appears to relate to being strung out on heroin. The lines 'Heading for the overload / Splattered on the dirty road' for instance, and the chorus stating that his character can only 'get his rocks off' while he's dreaming/sleeping. A particularly sharp line is 'The sunshine bores the daylights out of me', which again suggests the nocturnal life of the junkie. In the middle of the song is a strange, dreamy sounding bridge, with an almost underwater effect applied to Jagger's vocals via a phasing effect. Bobby Keys and Nicky Hopkins are prominent on this one as well. A great opening.

'Rip This Joint' (Jagger, Richards)

The fastest song on the album, and one of the fastest in the entire Stones history, this is simultaneously a nod back to their Chuck Berry roots and a precursor and inspiration for the punk movement some four years later. Wyman does not feature on this track, and instead, upright bass is provided by Bill Plummer. Hopkins excels on piano, while Keys puts in another excellent solo (these two could almost have been band members at this time); Jim Price, somewhat unusually, plays the trombone here. Jagger's lyric is excellent, outlining a whistle-stop tour across the Southern states of the USA while also making reference to their customs hassles. Full of namechecks for cities, clever wordplay and some interesting character references ('Dick and Pat in ole DC' are then-President Richard Nixon and his wife Pat), it's addictive stuff. So full of energy is the track that Aerosmith vocalist Steven Tyler once said that the only way for him to feel the 'buzz' necessary to keep on his first detox cure was to listen to 'Rip This Joint'. Richards has said that Jagger didn't like the track, mainly because it was so fast it practically shredded his larynx while singing it!

'Shake Your Hips' (Slim Harpo)

A cover of a song written by Louisiana Blues legend Slim Harpo, the Stones rendition stays very close to the Harpo original, right down to Watts providing his accompaniment on the metal rim of his snare drum. A good rendition without really adding much in terms of originality, this is a good example of the whole album being better than all of the individual tracks, as this may be something of a throwaway in isolation, but it reinforces that swampy groove of the album as a whole, and continues to immerse the listener. Oh, and that riff at the beginning? Yep, I think ZZ Top may have been listening when they came up with 'La Grange' the following year...

'Casino Boogie' (Jagger, Richards)

Pure good-time blues boogie here, with no pretence to be anything else. Another song which has little of note about it yet finds the listener unconsciously tapping his foot by the time it wends towards its conclusion, again this is a perfect example of contributing more to the album than it consists of in isolation. There are two solos here, the first by Bobby Keys (again! Sign that man up, guys...) and the second by Mick Taylor, who contributes some excellent ad-libbed licks in the coda. The lyrics have no meaning, as they were generated by the William Burroughs 'cut-up' method, of cutting random words and phrases from a newspaper or some such, and picking them at random (David Bowie, of course, embraced this later in the decade) – so no, that line about Cannes may not be referring to anyone in particular!

'Tumbling Dice' (Jagger, Richards)

The only hit single from the album (number 5 in the UK and 7 in the US), this Side One closer is undoubtedly head and shoulders above much of the other material on the album in terms of individual song highlights. Opening with a classic Richards riff, it all comes together irresistibly behind Jagger's superbly delivered vocals in a way which defines as perfectly as any song in the Stones canon the strength of their unique louche swagger. Simply put, nobody can do this type of track quite like the Rolling Stones. No one.

Inspired by the gambling which went on most of the time at Nellcôte, and also a conversation with his housekeeper who happened to be a keen dice player herself, the lyrics deal with a womanising gambler, mixing sex and gambling in a way that the old bluesmen used to do as a regular trick. It is of course cleverly sequenced so that it follows the 'Casino' theme of the preceding track. For songs like this one and 'Rocks Off', among others on the record, Jagger requested specifically that he be lowered in the mix a little so that people would have to gain a full understanding of the songs through repeated listening, as he remembered doing himself with his beloved old blues records.

The rhythm section is interesting on this track. Firstly, once again Wyman is not present. He played on the track while they were working out the arrangement, but was not there for the actual recording session, and Mick Taylor handles the bass duties, as well as slide guitar (Jagger and Richards are both featured on rhythm guitar). Of greater interest perhaps is that this track is unique in the Stones catalogue for featuring two drummers. Charlie Watts handled the tricky drum parts with aplomb until around a minute from the end of the song when there is a 'breakdown' which reconvenes again in an extended 'outro'. He had what has been described as a 'mental block' about that part, and in the end, Jimmy Miller sat in and covered that final section. You can't see the join though!

Soulful backing vocals are provided by a trio of singers – Venetta Fields,

Clydie King and Sherlie Matthews – and once again Hopkins, Keys and Price are present. The song actually began life much earlier than the French sessions, as a Jagger composition called 'Good Time Women'. This was left unused for a couple of years until Richards reworked the music and Jagger came up with the final lyric. 'Good Time Women' was finally heard by the public in 2010 when a recording was used as a CD bonus track on an *Exile* reissue. It is serviceable in a raw sort of way, but let us say the transformation was significant...

'Sweet Virginia' (Jagger, Richards)

In which the Country Stones rear their head again, with this ramshackle sing-along – but very much modern Country, Bakersfield Country. This is far removed from a Grand Ole Opry, Nashville country sound, but the amazing thing is that it sounds so utterly and completely genuine that you'd never imagine for a minute that it's a gang of English guys in the south of France! The song opens with Richards playing the intro with Jagger on harmonica, and then Taylor takes over some superb lead acoustic playing while Watts uses brushes to accompany. There is a choir of various backing vocalists encouraging the sing-along element, among whom is alleged to be Dr John, the legendary New Orleans musician and composer of 'Walk on Gilded Splinters'. On the surface, the song is most certainly about drugs and various intoxicants, with references to heroin, speed, wine, pills and sundry others throughout, but it is hard to tell from the general atmosphere of the song whether this is a cautionary or celebratory tale! Whatever the intention, like all great songs it has transcended that by becoming a bar-room holler second to none, and also the chorus line of 'got to scrape the shit right off your shoes' has struck a chord with many, many people down the years seeking to rid themselves of some 'baggage' of whatever kind. Therein lies its real success.

'Torn and Frayed' (Jagger, Richards)

More country influence here, though this time much more in the vein of the country-rock pioneered by Keith's muse Gram Parsons. The song tells of a down-at-heel hobo-type rootless musician, going from one seedy venue to another with his coat 'torn and frayed', yet as soon as he plays it can 'steal your heart away'. There is also a nod toward getting hooked on prescription medication, with the verse about the Joe character, with his cough and 'the codeine to fix it'. It's another infectious song like its predecessor, nailing down a solid identity for this second side of the album of acoustic music with country roots. There is a great pedal steel guitar solo mid-song, which is contributed by Al Perkins, from Gram Parsons' band The Flying Burrito Brothers, while elsewhere Richards handles most of the guitar work, with Taylor chiming in with some lead work in the final 30 seconds or so. Taylor also handles bass duties on this one (with great aplomb) as Wyman is again absent, and Nicky Hopkins and Jim Price contribute some piano and organ respectively which is vital to the overall sound. A popular track among many fans.

'Sweet Black Angel' (Jagger, Richards)

The subject of this country-blues protest ballad is Angela Davis, a black American civil activist who was arrested for and finally acquitted of involvement in an attempted hostage-taking at a California court, which resulted in the deaths of four people, including the judge. She was acquitted and released just after *Exile* appeared, but when the song was written she was being held pending trial for conspiracy to murder and was something of a political cause celebre at the time (witness John Lennon's song 'Angela', also released in 1972 on his *Some Time In New York City* album.

The protest element of the lyrics can often overshadow the song itself in this case, not least because overtly political songs are rarities in the Stones output. In fact, it is a pleasant and well-played ballad which makes its point succinctly. Jagger's overly affected 'African-American' accent, while undoubtedly well-meaning as a homage, comes across rather heavy-handed and in retrospect the song would have been better served without affectations such as 'She countin' up de minutes, she countin' up de days' from the Kent born and bred singer. No Wyman again here, but no bass either. No drums either, but there is percussion from Watts, Miller and Dr John sideman Richard 'Didymus' Washington (on marimba), the latter credited as 'Amyl Nitrate' (a fact that he apparently was not best pleased by).

'Loving Cup' (Jagger, Richards)

Closing the side is this uplifting folk-rock ballad – for want of a better description – which manages to straddle a very skilful tightrope. Lyrically it is loaded with sexual innuendo, from the 'loving cup' itself onward (or should we say 'downward', as the wordplay is often at a fairly base level). This could easily lead to it coming across as gauche and artless in lesser hands, and yet the grace with which the song is arranged and performed lends it an unashamedly romantic air. Not an easy balance to pull off, but especially in the bridge section with its transcendent 'What a beautiful buzz' lines, one that is effortlessly achieved. Mick Taylor does not appear on this one, but the real unsung star of the show is Nicky Hopkins, whose piano holds the whole house of cards together. The song was originally worked on a couple of years earlier, with the title 'Give Me A Drink', and one listen to it on the *Exile* CD reissue confirms just how much Hopkins contributed to the final version.

'Happy' (Jagger, Richards)

More than any other, this Side Three opener was, is and will always be Keith's signature song. And for good reason – when the basic track was recorded at Nellcôte he was the only Stone present. Bill Wyman, thoroughly frustrated, demotivated and, essentially, sulking, had rented a yacht and disappeared off on it for five days, thus making his feelings on the sessions abundantly clear. Jagger, Watts and Taylor were also absent on this particular afternoon when Keith announced he had an idea for a song. He started playing the guitar parts in the basement studio, and when Miller joined in on drums and the ever-faithful Bobby Keys also dropped in to contribute, the whole thing was worked out and recorded in a single afternoon. Overdubs were added later, with piano and an extra horn section, but Jagger only contributed his (distinctive, it has to be said) backing vocals at a much later date in Los Angeles. Richards handles bass duties. Thus, on the final release, The Glimmer Twins (as Jagger and Richards had by now become commonly known) were the only Rolling Stones members to feature, with Richards himself handling all of the lead and rhythm guitars as well as bass and lead vocals. Keys said later, in his book Every Night's A Saturday Night, that he thought he might have deserved a writing credit for helping to come up with the main riff, but he also admitted that at the end of the day he had simply taken part in a jam session. One thing is for sure though – if he had received a credit it would have been more relevant than Jagger's since he wasn't even in the room.

'Turd on the Run' (Jagger, Richards)

Back to the vitriolic Jagger lyrically here for this oddly titled song. He appears to be berating an ex-lover for a catalogue of betrayals she has visited upon him as he tried everything to make her stay, only to be left as she has gone with the diamond rings and left him 'with disease'. Essentially, he then voices his desire to murder her. It's a cheery tale.

The music accompanying this tirade is two and a half minutes of rockabilly blues on amphetamines, with a frantically sawing rhythm keeping on and on and on without let up. Subtle it is not, and a sing-along feelgood piece it most certainly is not, but it does have its place in the overall sound of the album. Once again, as a stand-alone song this would be very weak, but on *Exile* it somehow works. The only parallel is the Beatles songs which somehow only work because they are on the *White Album*. Wyman is AWOL again, but Bill Plummer fills in, frantically hammering away on an upright bass amid the carnage.

'Ventilator Blues' (Jagger, Richards, Taylor)

An actual credit for someone outside the Glimmer Twins axis, as Mick Taylor gets in on the action for his one and only writing credit with the band. A heavy, churning blues-rock track, it rolls along with a mid-paced, relentlessly crushing intensity driven by Taylor's masterful slide guitar riff. The inspiration for the track was the single, malfunctioning, small fan set high in one of the walls in the sweltering basement studio. The humidity became so great that Taylor was having to stop to retune his guitar periodically, and tempers were getting short. Jagger fused that feeling brilliantly into a lyric describing situations in which people are going to blow unless they somehow get 'a ventilator'. The effect of these lyrics, his remorseless delivery and the grinding musical beast surrounding it all causes the listener to feel they are stressed, sweating and irritable with the pressure about to take over. It's remarkable in its way. It would be difficult to take for more than its three-and-a-half minute duration, but as it is, it is perfect, fading out as Jagger repeats again and again 'Don't fight it'. A remarkable piece of work.

'I Just Want to See His Face' (Jagger, Richards)

Emerging directly as a fade-in from 'Ventilator Blues', this hypnotic mantra-style piece emerged from a three-man jam between Jagger, Watts and Mick Taylor on bass, with Jagger essentially improvising the words. Electric piano was added later – Bobby Whitlock has claimed that he definitely played this, but he is not credited on the sleeve. It's an oddly hypnotic track and a very unusual one for the Stones, but not really a highlight on the album. Incidentally, however, Tom Waits cites this as his favourite Stones track – so make of that what you will...

'Let It Loose' (Jagger, Richards)

Sounding from the title as if it is going to be a typical ragged Stones rocker, this Side Three closer is anything but. A stirring, emotional song which builds to a crescendo, it owes more to soul and gospel, with a choir of backing vocalists (definitely including Dr John this time) giving it that gospel feel. Mick Taylor is not present on this one, but once again Nicky Hopkins is the hero, with one of the greatest piano performances you will ever hear on a rock album, anchoring the song and accentuating its build up in power throughout. The moment when Bobby Keys' saxophone break enters is also stirring stuff. Jagger has claimed that he remembers Richards writing the lyrics, but that he is unsure what they are about, which has led many to read into it that Keith's feelings about Mick's imminent marriage to Bianca may have been a strong element ('See that girl on your arm / All dressed up to do you harm'). However, this is conjecture as Richards has never even confirmed whether he indeed wrote it.

'All Down the Line' (Jagger, Richards)

The fourth and final side of the album opens with a straight-ahead burst of pure rock and roll energy, cut straight from the same cloth as 'Brown Sugar' and the like. A regular in Stones shows for almost all of their tours since, it is a perfect live number, bristling with energy and momentum. Richards and Taylor work brilliantly together here, with Keith's rock-solid rhythm playing perfectly complemented by Taylor's excellent slide guitar part. It's interesting to note that, despite the breadth of material included on the album, three out of its four sides open with a straight-ahead propulsive rocker – the exception being Side Two of course, with 'Sweet Virginia'. Appearing on backing vocals here is Kathi McDonald, who had previously been one of the 'Ikettes' with Ike & Tina Turner, and also sang with Big Brother and the Holding Company after Janis Joplin's departure.

'Stop Breaking Down' (Johnson)

A cover of a song by the legendary bluesman (and late-night crossroads visitor) Robert Johnson is up next. Originally titled 'Stop Breaking Down Blues' by Johnson, the Stones' version arranges the song quite differently on this occasion. Jagger is a dominant force here, contributing rhythm guitar and some brilliant harmonica as well as vocals, in the surprising absence of Keith

Richards. Ian Stewart is on piano this time out, but the real star, aside from Jagger's harmonica, is Mick Taylor's masterful slide guitar part. The song is rocked-up beyond anything that could have been envisioned at the time of the original, and all told is one of the band's better blues adaptations.

'Shine A Light' (Jagger, Richards)

This bittersweet gospel-infused song was written by Jagger as a sort of tribute to Brian Jones, a snapshot of his decline and fall. It manages to be both solemn and uplifting at the same time. Neither Richards nor Watts was present on this recording, with Jimmy Miller again filling in for Watts and Mick Taylor taking the laurels for his guitar part, injected with audible feeling and emotion. Indeed, he would himself name it as one of his favourite tracks on the album, and it is hard to argue with that. Billy Preston's piano and organ highlights the gospel feeling of the track. There was an earlier version of the song worked on as far back as the *Let It Bleed* sessions, at which time it was called 'Get A Line on You'. It was also worked on during the *Sticky Fingers* sessions, before finally reaching its apex here.

'Soul Survivor' (Jagger, Richards)

The final song on the album, the upbeat, rocking 'Soul Survivor' tells the story, in a literal sense, of a group of sailors heading for destruction. However, metaphorically it is surely about the decaying of a relationship 'on the rocks' and could even be seen as referencing the tensions between Jagger and Richards during this album, as they often seemed to lock horns over the true leadership of the band. It's a good song on which to end, with once more Nicky Hopkins' piano keeping things afloat (to continue the nautical theme). All of the band are present on this closing track except, once again, the unhappy Wyman and bass duties are handled by Mick Taylor.

On reflection, when evaluating this album, one thing which becomes abundantly clear is the feeling of total artistic freedom that the Stones had at this point. Known, of course, as 'the greatest rock and roll band in the world', they could nevertheless take on soul, gospel, country, blues or folk – essentially, whatever the Stones did was deemed 'cool'. They were, at this time, the ultimate rock and roll outlaws, and with that image intact anything they turned their hand to had that armour-plated 'Stones touch' to it. Not that being regarded as effortlessly cool meant the same as being regarded as always good, indeed *Exile* suffered quite a negative critical reception when it appeared and was not an immediate massive seller. However, after 'Tumbling Dice' the sales momentum built up and the album reached Number One on both sides of the Atlantic. It also began growing in reputation over the years, and by the end of the decade was regularly looked on as one of the greatest rock albums of the decade. Take a straw poll of Stones fans even today, and the majority of votes for their best album will likely be either for *Exile* or *Sticky Fingers*.

Goats Head Soup (1973)

Personnel:
Mick Jagger: vocals, guitar, harmonica, piano
Keith Richards: guitar, vocals, bass
Mick Taylor: guitar, bass, vocals
Bill Wyman: bass
Charlie Watts: drums and percussion
With
Nicky Hopkins: piano
Ian Stewart: piano
Billy Preston: clavinet, piano
Bobby Keys: Saxophone
Jim Horn: Saxophone

Record Label: Rolling Stones Records
Recorded: November 1972-June 1973, produced by Jimmy Miller.
Release Date: August 1973.
Highest chart places: UK: 1, US: 1
Running time: 46:56

Album Facts:

Before recording began on this album, Keith and Anita had managed to throw a spanner in the works by once again falling foul of the authorities. Unsurprisingly, during the recording of *Exile*, the police had been keeping something of a close eye on activities at the Nellcôte property, and ultimately – largely based on testimony supplied by disgruntled employees apparently, but also presumably from their observation that the property was a veritable hive of shady characters – arrived at the conclusion that the couple had been heroin trafficking. Whether this was right or wrong, it did pose something of a problem, but Prince Rupert Loewenstein, the Stones' financial advisor and business manager since 1968, managed to secure a guarantee of freedom for Keith and Anita, as long as they left France forthwith and continued to rent Nellcôte as a sign of good faith. Note that Loewenstein was, in fact, an actual Prince, from the Bavarian royal house, and his full name was in fact – pull up a chair for this one – Rupert Louis Ferdinand Frederick Constantine Lofredo Leopold Herbert Maximilian Hubert John Henry zu Löwenstein-Wertheim-Freudenberg, Count of Loewenstein-Scharffeneck. Beats 'Michael Philip Jagger', doesn't it? Still, the Stones affectionately, and utterly disrespectfully, dubbed him Rupie The Groupie, which I imagine was easier for all concerned.

In June the Stones headed over to the USA for the band's 1972 America tour, a jaunt which has passed into legend as a byword for excess, hedonism, riots and newspaper headlines. It was unofficially known as the 'Stones Touring Party' (STP) or the Cocaine and Tequila Sunrise Tour. Keith surprised everyone by actually surviving this little road trip, perhaps because before it commenced, he had completed his first detox programme at a clinic in Vevey, Switzerland, where he and Anita were now living. It would be the first of several such occurrences! For now though, in November 1972, the five Stones arrived at their recording destination of choice, Kingston, Jamaica, with Richards announcing 'It was about the only country in the world which would let us all in to work! The only place in Europe that would have me was Switzerland...'

Taking up residence in the Terra Nova Hotel, once the family home of Island Records chief Chris Blackwell, the band elected to record the album at Byron Lee's Dynamic Sound Studios in downtown Kingston, where Jimmy Cliff and Bob Marley had recently recorded the albums *The Harder They Come* and *Catch A Fire*, respectively. Now, downtown Kingston is a hazardous place for the outsider to visit, particularly for white Europeans (a fact the author can personally attest to!), and it did not escape the band's attention that when they were driven to the studio each day they were not only greeted by imposing double gates guarded by a man with a shotgun but also that the drumkits and amps in the studio were nailed to the floor. To prevent theft and/or bootlegging the tapes of the recordings were transferred out of the studio marked up as 'Muddy Waters'. Despite all of this, or knowing him, perhaps because of it, Keith developed a love for the country and the music and would spend a lot of time there in the future. Still, back to *Goats Head Soup*, and let's see how that man Mr Jagger has been upsetting record company people again...

After the recording was complete, the tapes were sent to Atlantic Records chief Ahmet Ertegun for his approval (although it was the band's own label, it was distributed by Atlantic, so they still held a number of cards, so to speak). When he heard the album's final track 'Starfucker', complete with not only very explicit female sexual references but also tales of a groupie's planned or successful exploits with Steve McQueen and John Wayne, Ertegun first reached for the smelling salts and then for the phone. A *Beggars Banquet* style stand-off situation erupted, with Ertegun insisting the record would never go out with that song on it and Jagger refusing to budge, claiming they would put out what they wanted on their own label. Last time it was just a toilet wall – this time the record company were actually fearing charges of distributing pornography! You always got a story with the Stones...

Ultimately, with the track renamed 'Star Star' and other compromises in place (see track details below), the album went ahead. Helped by the massive worldwide success of the single 'Angie', the album – despite some mixed reviews – topped the charts once again on both sides of the Atlantic. Deservedly so, as it is an excellent, and very underrated album, containing some of Mick Taylor's finest work. Many progressive rock fans' favourite Stones album, which admittedly is not the core demographic, Jimmy Miller is producer for the final time here as, severely affected by his drug habits, he had become a shadow of his former self. Hard to believe it, but this is the first Stones album since *Satanic Majesties* not to feature a cover song and the first since *Aftermath* to be entirely Jagger/Richards penned.

Album Cover:

This is another strange one, even by Stones standards. The slightly odd album title is actually inspired by the Jamaican dish Mannish Water, which is a soup not only made from the head of a goat but also other parts including its genitals. (Mmm. Tasty). Despite this fact, neither goats – heads or otherwise – nor soup are anywhere to be seen on the outer cover, which has the five Stones photographed in a surreal manner across its gatefold panels. Mick's head is on the front, veiled in a creepy manner against a halo of yellow light, as if perhaps dead (the intention of photographer David Bailey was to make him look like Katherine Hepburn apparently, for some unfathomable reason), while Keith's head adorns the rear cover, blackened, as if charred into the yellow background. He definitely looks as if he could be dead. The three 'others', as the non-Glimmer Twin Stones, unfortunately, were always seen, share the inner gatefold in similarly distorted fashion (Wyman resembles Keith, albeit green, while the other two more closely resemble Jagger). Bizarre though this tableau may be, it may be a blessing that this final design dreamed up by Jagger and Bailey was used instead of the original design, by renowned left-field thinkers Hipgnosis, which had the Stones prancing around as centaurs and minotaurs. One can only shudder at how ghastly that may have been. There was also an inner sleeve which featured photos of some of the guest musicians on the album, as well as the credits, and an insert on which the titular goat finally made an appearance – at the band's insistence – as a head floating in a most unappetising reddish soup.

'Dancing with Mr D' (Jagger, Richards)

The opening track on the album rides in on an insistent, sinuous, funk-rock groove which seems to become more hypnotic as the song progresses. Its snakelike feel perfectly matches Jagger's brilliantly worded ode to the grim reaper (as Mr D is, of course, Death). Across the three dark yet highly literate verses we see him describing encounters with Death in both male and female personas, and also musing on how his own final 'dance' with Mr D might take place ('A drink of Belladonna on a Toussaint night', as one memorable line has it). The main guitar part here is laid down by Keith, while Mick Taylor supplies some slide work and also bass, covering for the once again absent Bill Wyman, who really did seem to be less than fully engaged at this time. Good old Nicky Hopkins is on piano again, while some unidentified backing vocalists do an understated job. There is an official promo video for the track, which makes for odd viewing, as Jagger, heavily made up, camps it up mercilessly in a gold lame suit and ill-advised buttock-shaking gestures that make him appear like some kind of large, defeathered, flightless bird. Keith looks cool as always, Wyman pretends it's him playing while looking bored and Mick Taylor preens happily in a ladies' hat looking more suitable for Ascot. The audio-only option is preferable! An excellent track, albeit one which probably wrong-footed people waiting for *Exile* Part Two.

'100 Years Ago' (Jagger, Richards)

This song sees Jagger looking back nostalgically to a simpler and more carefree time ('Mary and I, we would sit upon a gate, just gazin' at some dragon in the sky / What tender days, we had no secrets hid away, well, it seemed about a hundred years ago'), while contrasting it with the present, and all his friends wearing 'worried smiles'. He asks the question 'Don't you think it's sometimes wise not to grow up?', which is one of those seemingly throwaway lines which resonate with the listener, something that Jagger was extremely gifted at doing. Billy Preston drives the song along with the clavinet, giving it a slightly funky feel reminiscent of Stevie Wonder's 'Superstition' (which also uses the instrument prominently), but the real star here is Mick Taylor, who covers all of the guitar parts as Richards fills in on bass for – yes, you guessed it – the absent Bill Wyman. Seriously Bill, show up now and again, could you?

Taylor takes a couple of solos in the song. The first is mixed lower underneath Jagger's vocal midway through, but then after a slow bridging section, a lengthy fast-paced coda brings him in again, using his wah-wah pedal to great effect as he effortlessly slashes across the music like strokes of Zorro's blade. This is the real Mick Taylor, and when he has the chance to cut loose it is a joy to hear. A great, if lesser known track, it was played live on the Stones' 1973 tour, but never since.

'Coming Down Again' (Jagger, Richards)

Very much a Richards song here, this weary-sounding ballad is sung by him. There are clear references to the Keith-Anita-Brian triangle in the lyrics, but overall this simply exudes heroin listlessness and regret. The oft-repeated 'Coming down again ... Where are all my friends?' has an inescapable 'after the party' feel to it which it is only too clear is something of an area of great familiarity for Keith. Laconic and firmly funereally-paced, the song subverts expectations throughout, never growing to a climax and even having a sax solo (from Keys, of course) when all the signs point to it being a Taylor mournful guitar solo. In fact, Taylor doesn't even play guitar on this track, instead handling the bass duties instead of you-know-who (seriously, what was he doing at this time?), and the wah-wah guitar which sounds like him is, in fact, Keith. Jagger only contributes backing vocals to this one, and once again the joint writing credit appears absurd. Hopkins is again on piano, particularly at the beginning where he introduces the song, followed soon by Taylor's exceptional bass line. It was never played live.

'Doo Doo Doo Doo Doo (Heartbreaker)' (Jagger, Richards)

This bizarrely titled track (it comes from the sound of the backing vocalists on the song) is one of Jagger's grittiest lyrics, telling the tale of two incidents set in New York City, which are fictionalised but may have their basis in factual events. Firstly, there is the tale of a young boy shot through the heart in error by the police, while the second, equally tragic, play thread concerns a ten-year-old girl dying of a drug overdose in an alleyway. While the recording was taking place, there was a highly publicised account of a police shooting of a ten-year-old boy in Queens when they mistakenly identified him as a jewel thief, despite the fact that he was with his father at the time. Clearly wishing to make a point about the violent and highly charged climate in the US, and especially NYC, at that time, it is highly likely that the story was extrapolated to form the basis of the two incidents in the song. The title is gimmicky and, to be honest, does not serve the song well as it gives it the air of being much lighter and more throwaway in tone than it actually is. Simply 'Heartbreaker' would have been much better. The NYPD is not well represented in the lyrics (such as the chorus part 'Heartbreaker, with your .44'), and there were claims that they refused to provide security at the band's NYC appearances for some time, but this is unsubstantiated.

Once again Wyman is somewhere else doing crosswords or playing table tennis or whatever he was doing, and Richards plays bass on the track. Taylor plays all the guitars, and it is he and the horn section (arranged by Jim Price) who are the real stars of this one, though Jagger is impressive also and Billy Preston's clavinet gives the track a funky edge. Interestingly, in their original late-1970s incarnation, '80s new wave-electronica band Japan used to feature this track prominently in their live shows.

'Angie' (Jagger, Richards)

Hang out the flags to celebrate – Bill Wyman appears on this song! Released as a single in August 1973, it only reached Number 5 in the UK, but topped the charts in the USA and also in many other countries around the world. A superbly crafted ballad, delicately and emotionally sung by Jagger, the music was entirely by Keith with the lyrics a combination of the two – though believed to be more from Jagger. The identity of 'Angie' is unclear, Richards has at different times claimed it to be about his newly-born daughter Dandelion Angela (in the *Jump Back* compilation sleevenotes) and to be a random name not referring to anyone in particular (in his autobiography, Life). Putting the cat among the pigeons still further, in a 1990 TV interview Angie Bowie claimed that around 1972 she arrived home to find her husband and Jagger in bed together and that Mick dedicated the song to her to appease her. It should be noted, however, that Jagger has always denied this. The most likely explanation is that Angie was a conglomeration of different women since different parts of the lyric seem to relate particularly well too, for example, Mick and Marianne or Keith and Anita. The closing 'Angie, Angie... They can't say we never tried' in particular is heart-wrenchingly sublime.

Richards and Taylor play terrifically interwoven acoustic guitar parts on the song, with the very beginning, by Keith, having a resemblance to the Eagles' later 'Hotel California'. The strings on this one are arranged by Nicky Harrison, while Hopkins' piano is again crucial. It seems odd now, considering the quality of the song and the Stones' excellent track record with ballads all the way back to 'As Tears Go By', but this was one of the tracks which critics used to beat the album, claiming it was too heavy on that type of material. Essentially, many people wanted another *Exile*. They didn't get it and lashed out at what was a quite different, yet no less brilliant, album.

'Silver Train' (Jagger, Richards)

Released as the B-side to the 'Angie' single, this track was originally recorded as far back as 1970 but not officially released. Johnny Winter, however, heard it and included it on his *Still Alive and Well* album released in March 1973. Following this (and likely as a result of Winter's version), the Stones revisited the track and recorded this final take of it. A country-tinged fast rocker with some neat slide work from Taylor, while powerfully played it is less distinguished from a songwriting perspective than other tracks on *Goats Head Soup* and is arguably the weakest song on the album. In addition to vocals, Jagger plays rhythm guitar and some rather pedestrian harmonica. Once again, Wyman failed to board the train.

'Hide Your Love' (Jagger, Richards)

Proof if it were needed that, despite the greater polish and sheen on most of this album, the Blues Stones never really went away. This one is enlivened particularly by the brilliant guitar work of Taylor, which is so good that Richards steps back to rhythm guitar to give him the spotlight, even though it is in a style at which he is himself so adept. There is nothing deep or meaningful beyond that in the song, it is just an infectious and expertly performed 12-bar boogie-blues. Note that as well as their love, they also hid Bill Wyman, who is again conspicuous by his absence, covered for here by Richards.

'Winter' (Jagger, Richards)

The standout track on the album, and one of the highlights of the band's entire career, 'Winter' is, without doubt, the single most overlooked track in the Stones catalogue. The first track recorded after the band arrived in Jamaica, it features a beautifully delivered, evocative Jagger lyric conjuring up the atmosphere of a long, cold winter and nostalgic feelings of lost love so perfectly that listening on headphones can almost make it seem as if opening the curtains would see snow falling outside. Indeed, this is all Jagger – or rather Jagger and Taylor, who were apparently the real co-writers of the song – and despite his usual writing credit Keith does not even play on the track, and has admitted that great as it was, it had nothing to do with him. The departure of Taylor after the next album would be partly blamed on his consistent lack of songwriting recognition, and who can blame him? This proved to be a very costly decision by the Glimmer Twins, as Taylor's departure left a huge hole, which some believe, despite the loyal Ron Wood's sterling service, has never been entirely filled.

The song builds in beautiful fashion, up until around the 3:20 mark when

Taylor launches into a solo which simply mesmerises as it soars and weeps. This is the best guitar work ever seen within the band, despite Keith's extraordinary eccentric genius, and it drags the song up to another plane, where it remains until its conclusion, thanks to Nicky Harrison's transcendent string arrangement, which meshes with Jagger's vocal and spirals away until the end. And still, many people have never even heard this song!

Jagger throws in one of his enigmatic phrases with 'I'm burning my bell, book and candle' evoking the arcane Catholic exorcism ritual, and follows it up with 'and the restoration plays have all gone round' – simultaneously displaying his extremely literate lyrical bent and also his lack of throwing in a line or two to have people comparing interpretations. Jagger supports Taylor on rhythm guitar in Keith's absence, while the piano is clearly Nicky Hopkins, as the 'no minor chords please' Ian Stewart would be way out of his comfort zone with this stuff. The actor Bill Nighy has declared this as one of his favourite tracks on the BBC Desert Island Discs show, and he's not wrong. Classic.

And hey – Bill Wyman's back! He appears on the final three songs on the album now.

'Can You Hear the Music' (Jagger, Richards)

Another hugely underrated piece. Opening with an atmospheric tinkling of bells with meandering flute, it appears as if it is going to take us back to something from *Satanic Majesties* and the Brian Jones days, but it quickly turns into a swampy, voodoo-laden churning mid-paced rocker driven by a great, insistent rhythm section, courtesy of the rock-solid Watts and Wyman. Jagger is almost trance-like as he hails the universal power of music over the hypnotic beat and serpentine flute of Jim Horn which conjure up a ritual invocation of some kind. It's addictive, irresistibly sucking the listener into its groove. Richards is responsible for the thick, soupy rhythm guitar sound (probably using the wah-wah), but Taylor is on hand to sprinkle a little bit of fairy dust in the background at the uplifting 'Love is a mystery' sections. Interestingly, it is one of the relatively small number of Stones songs which has never been covered by any other artist. Probably because they couldn't. This one is definitely made by the playing rather than the songwriting, 'The singer not the song', as one might say.

'Star Star' (Jagger, Richards)

... as it was ultimately called in its compromise form for Atlantic Records! We have already dealt with the controversy around the title and lyrics of the song, but how does it cut the mustard musically? Answer – unstoppably! Opening with one of Keith's trademark Chuck Berry riffs, it seems at first as if it is going to be a lightweight, if fun, basic rocker. Then in a masterstroke, at the beginning of the second verse, Bill Wyman belatedly enters the fray on his Fender Mustang bass, and suddenly the song is relaunched completely. It drives along, with Jagger at his lasciviously lip-smacking best, delivering lines such as 'Your tricks with fruit was kinda cute' in the way that only he can. The chorus is incredibly simplistic, containing the words 'star fucker' an impressive twelve times in a single chorus iteration, yet it is utterly infectious and almost impossible to resist bellowing it along with the highly enthused Jagger. Unless you happen to be a vicar, in which case probably advised to listen alone.

The line 'Ali McGraw got mad at you for giving head to Steve McQueen' appeared loud and proud after McQueen happily gave his permission for it, but on early pressings the line 'you're gonna get John Wayne before he dies' has the word 'Wayne' censored clumsily by a huge echo invading the mix for a split second – not just on the vocal, but on everything! Today, conversely, it is hard to get hold of the censored version, which was soon dropped. There is, however, a censored South African version which is hilarious, as it interjects a huge buzz on every use of the offending word, so while John Wayne gets away unscathed, in an absurd butchering job we are treated to a triumphant chorus of 'You're a star BUZZ star BUZZ star BUZZ star BUZZ star'. Over sixty times throughout the song! It's worse than it sounds...

It is interesting to note that, despite the hysterical protests of Island Records about the song, when they released a four-track jukebox EP to promote the album, have a guess what was Track One, Side One? Yep, that's right. A testament to the track's quality and all in all a fine way to close a much-undervalued album.

Related Song:

'Criss Cross Man' (Jagger, Richards)

Recorded during the album sessions and originally intended for the album, this heavy grooving funk-rock track would have made an excellent addition to the album, and certainly superior to 'Hide Your Love' which eventually replaced it. Mick Taylor's wah-wah drenched lead guitar and Nicky Hopkins' great keyboard work combine to enmesh the track in a great, funky wall of sound. It's amazing that this track (also known as 'Criss Cross Mind' and 'Save Me') was never officially released. It certainly would have fit onto the next album particularly well.

It's Only Rock 'n' Roll (1974)

Personnel:
Mick Jagger: vocals, guitar
Keith Richards: guitar, vocals, bass
Mick Taylor: guitar, bass
Bill Wyman: bass, synthesizer
Charlie Watts: drums and percussion
With
Nicky Hopkins: piano
Ian Stewart: piano
Billy Preston: clavinet, piano, organ
Ray Cooper: percussion
Ron Wood: guitar
Kenney Jones: drums

Record Label: Rolling Stones Records
Recorded: November 1973-May 1973, produced by Jagger/Richards (credited as The Glimmer Twins)
Release Date: October 1974.
Highest chart places: UK: 2, US: 1
Running time: 48:26

Album facts:

Jimmy Miler was out with this one, with Jagger and Richards taking over the production duties. In fact, they chose this point to make their nickname public, and are credited on the album as 'The Glimmer Twins' for this role. The album was to be Mick Taylor's last, and it was an unsettled one for him; having missed the start of the sessions with health problems, he had several run-ins with the rest of the band during the subsequent recording. Some of this was down to his undervalued songwriting input, as we have already seen. The exception to the recording sessions was the title track, which had been conceived, and a basic track recorded, during a jam between Jagger and The Faces while Ron Wood was recording his solo album, *I've Got My Own Album To Do*, at his home The Wick, in Richmond, where he had installed a studio. He brought the basic track (which features Ron Wood on guitar, Kenney Jones on drums and Willie Weeks on bass) to the Stones and they were impressed. Some parts were overdubbed but some were left, as we will see. This, of course, paved the way for Wood to join the Stones as Mick Taylor's replacement after this album, a post which he still holds today.

Album Cover:

The somewhat self-aggrandising cover painting for the album, by Belgian artist Guy Peelaert, depicts the Stones descending a wide, red-carpeted stairway surrounded by hordes of adoring Grecian nymphs! Jagger, naturally, is front and centre. It was clear that the intent now was to literally paint the band as bona fide 'rock gods', having ascended Mount Olympus to superstardom. It makes for an eye-catching image if nothing else (and does not feature the band name or album title). Behind Jagger, who appears in a strangely mid-dance pose dressed in a cream suit and bare chest, Watts sports a casual upper-class outfit featuring lapel flower and open white scarf, Taylor also has a scarf but wrapped around his neck with an overcoat, Richards is in a strangely overly-tight red suit, with straining buttons visible, while Wyman appears as a sort of waistcoated gentleman farmer. It is an odd depiction, to say the least! If the style seems familiar, it is because Peelaert also painted David Bowie's famed *Diamond Dogs* album cover, released in the same year. The inner sleeve featured credits on one side and, like *Goats Head Soup* before it, photos of some of the guest musicians and engineering staff featured on the album.

The rear of the album, also by Peelaert, showed the same staircase empty and carpetless, with the wall at the top adorned with graffiti bearing the album title and the word 'Stones'. Before the album's release, graffiti bearing the words 'It's Only Rock 'n' Roll' appeared overnight in locations around London. The Stones, naturally given the illegality of the act, denied all knowledge of this and refuted the idea that it was an advertising campaign. Obviously, nobody believed them.

'If You Can't Rock Me' (Jagger, Richards)

A super-tight, aggressive rocker with a funky groove to it, this is the perfect album opener for an album which will prove to once again showcase a variety of musical avenues. Jagger's lyric, concerning being onstage and surveying the various girls in the audience, appears to be a fairly obvious one ('if you can't rock me then somebody will'), but some have perceived deeper meaning to the song, relating to the band's growing disenchantment with the rock and roll lifestyle, and Jagger's own commentary on his ongoing marriage to Bianca. Whatever the truth, it's not too important as the music is what drives this one, and it drives it powerfully and rhythmically. Richards again plays bass on this one, and to add insult to injury even takes a bass solo in a funky mid-song break – if Wyman was actually asked not to play at this time, rather than simply being absent, it does beg the question as to why he would have put up with it. History does not, however, record the reason for his absence on this occasion. Mick Taylor gives us some nice lead playing with his last guitar solo recorded with the band – the only song he recorded after this one was 'Fingerprint File', which did not include a guitar solo.

'Ain't Too Proud to Beg' (Whitfield, Holland)

The Stones do The Temptations, with this somewhat unexpected cover of that band's 1966 hit, written by Norman Whitfield and Eddie Holland. It's a curious hybrid of rock and soul, with Richards' slashing guitar chords giving it the former influence, while the funky bedrock of Wyman and Watts anchor it in the latter. Mick Taylor is nowhere to be seen on this one, and Keith takes the – rather perfunctory – guitar solo. In truth, it falls between the two stools and satisfies neither, and it's strange that this token throwback to the band's '60s cover work should occupy a place on an album which would still be 45 minutes – and arguably stronger – without it. The promo video which was shot for the track is a hideous embarrassment, with Jagger camping it up mercilessly in an eye-watering shiny pink and green suit while the band look sheepish alongside him. Try watching it, but don't watch it twice.

'It's Only Rock 'n' Roll (But I Like It)' (Jagger, Richards)

We have already looked at the gestation of this sizeable hit single, from Jagger's jam with the Faces, but we have not looked into what happened when Mick arrived 'home' with it. Essentially, everyone liked it – except for Mick Taylor, who never cared for it, and plays no part in the eventual recording. Richards replaced all of the guitars except for a minor acoustic guitar part by Ron Wood which he let stay, and also some rhythm guitar provided by Jagger. The album sleeve credits Willie Weeks for bass, but the accepted story is that Bill Wyman actually overdubbed the bass part – though the drums remain Kenney Jones, as Watts simply couldn't improve on what he had played, which is ironic since he was trying to play in the style of Charlie when he recorded it! It's a good song, with an infectious chorus, a classic piece of lyrical 'sloganeering', and a lively performance by Jagger. The lyric, concerning him asking the audience whether it would satisfy them if he stabbed himself in the heart with his pen and spilt his blood in an onstage suicide, deal sardonically with the seemingly insatiable demands the band seemed to be experiencing by now. As a lyric, it works well, but crucially it also sounds good, and you don't need to think about the meaning to enjoy it.

The promotional clip, which was played on BBC's Top of the Pops programme, bizarrely shows the band (including the non-participatory Taylor) in a sort of plastic tent filling with soap bubbles while they play on dressed, to a man, in sailor suits! In actual fact, this strange choice of attire was a last minute decision when, unhappy about having their clothes ruined, a costume of some kind was suggested and quickly agreed to. They probably weren't expecting five matching sailor suits to be produced, but there it was. The audio is different from the album version, with Jagger doing a new vocal take, and the guitar work sounds different as well, so it may be that Mick Taylor played on this occasion. Indeed, Taylor appears to be having fun, while Keith models a large gap in his rapidly deteriorating teeth, but all bets are off at the three-minute mark when the suds make their entrance. Pretty quickly the band are playing up to their necks – except for the unfortunate Watts who, being seated, quickly disappears below the deluge, and at one point can actually be seen waving his drumstick above his head as if signalling that he is in distress! Only the Stones could get away with this sort of nonsense and make it look cool, which somehow, they did.

'Till the Next Goodbye' (Jagger, Richards)

The first ballad on the album and an overlooked, if rather lovely, song. Featuring Jagger and Taylor on acoustic guitars and Keith on electric slide, Mick weaves a wistfully nostalgic yet ultimately regretful tale looking back on a love which seemingly cannot be rekindled, even by his lover's somewhat bizarre New Orleans concoction of cider vinegar and elderberry wine! The line 'Yeah, a movie house on Forty-Second Street / Ain't a very likely place for you and I to meet' is possibly a wry in-joke, as the movie-houses on that particular New York thoroughfare at that point in time would almost all have been exclusively showing porn films! Never performed live, nor compiled, the song is another understated Stones country-ballad in the 'Wild Horses' mode and deserves rather more attention than it gets. Once again, there is an official promo for this, but on this occasion, Jagger resists the awkward prancing in favour of simply singing the song with a guitar, and it is the better for it.

'Time Waits For No One' (Jagger, Richards)

While 'Till the Next Goodbye' tends to be forgotten, even by fans, this exquisite track is rightfully acknowledged as a bona fide classic by the Stones cognoscenti, even if it is unknown by the public at large. With a classic Jagger lyric about the inevitable march of time and impermanence of everything in its inexorable wake ('Time can tear down a building, or destroy a woman's face'), the slightly jazzy tinge is highly influenced by Taylor, even if it is mainly Jagger's words and music. The first half of the track's six-and-a-half minute duration is beautifully constructed, but it is the second half which really ascends to another level. As Jagger finishes the singing, Mick Taylor comes in with a solo which is simply breath-taking. Very reminiscent of Carlos Santana, and remarkably recorded in a single take, this lengthy fretboard excursion sees him peeling off spirals of ascending and descending notes which seem to lead the rest of the band in a delicate rhythmic dance quite unlike anything else the Stones have recorded. It is the best thing on the album by some distance, and along with 'Winter', one of the band's two towering mid-'70s 'deep cuts'. Taylor himself has said it is his favourite Stones track. For the solo, he used a Fender Stratocaster augmented by a Synthi Hi-Fli guitar effects synthesizer to get the distinctive tone.

Sadly, the song would also play a large part in the departure of Taylor, who was led to believe that he would be receiving a deserved writing credit for it, only to find out the reality from journalist Nick Kent when the album came out ('He went silent for a second before muttering a curt "We'll see about that!" almost under his breath', Kent said later). The injustice of this was keenly felt by the guitarist and led to some significant bitterness. For his part, Richards, while lamenting Taylor's departure heavily, took the alternative view that while he was 'a fucking great guitar player', he believed Taylor would be better served if he 'stopped pissing about trying to be a songwriter, producer, bandleader'. These contrary views make the departure of Taylor after the album unsurprising in retrospect, sadly. The band have never played this song live, and it is very easy to imagine the reason for that is that Taylor would be simply irreplaceable on what is certainly his Stones signature piece.

'Luxury' (Jagger, Richards)

By contrast to the previous Jagger/Taylor construction, this opening track on Side Two is all Keith, at least musically. The band's first foray into reggae (or at least, a sort of rock/reggae crossover driven along by Keith's crunching guitar work). With a lyric about a man working for a Texan oil company and receiving what he perceives as a pittance in return, it's a bouncy, fun and very enjoyable number, which like 'Sweet Black Angel' before it is marred only by Jagger's insistence on lapsing into an absurd cod-Jamaican accent as soon as he encounters anything remotely Caribbean in flavour ('To keep you in de luxury', for heaven's sake). Despite these embarrassing vocal mannerisms, it is an enjoyable track for all that. Mick Taylor sits this one out, with Richards handling all of the guitar duties.

'Dance Little Sister' (Jagger, Richards)

Another song rooted in the Caribbean, with its reference to Frederick Street, which is the main street of Port of Spain, the capital of Trinidad and Tobago, but this time there is no concession to Caribbean musical influence, with Keith's grimy, distorted guitar leading the band through a full-throttle grinding heavy rock rave-up. It is clear that Jagger – assuming the lyrics are his – has spent time in that particular location, as he uses the Trinidadian terms 'basodee' and 'mamaguy', meaning 'drunk' and 'tease' respectively. Maybe there is a slight hint of filler, but it is a very entertaining piece of it nonetheless.

'If You Really Want to Be My Friend' (Jagger, Richards)

Ballad number three on the album, after 'Till the Next Goodbye' and 'Time Waits For No One', this time there is an overtly bluesy feel to the song. A little reminiscent of the classic Derek and The Dominos track 'Bell Bottom Blues', the song sees Jagger appealing to his partner to try to help repair their relationship before it is too late, leading to questions as to whether he is, in fact, referencing Bianca, who he had married three years earlier. Once again Mick Taylor steps in to take some of the limelight, with a short but exquisitely Clapton-esque guitar solo at around the three-and-a-half minute mark really ramping the song up. For a band who have never really been applauded to any great degree for their ballads, the Stones were proving themselves masters of the form, with three very different examples on this album, all of which hit the mark squarely.

'Short and Curlies' (Jagger, Richards)

More blues influence here, this time in a boogie-woogie, good time rock format. Titled, of course, from the expression 'to have somebody by the short and curlies', meaning to be under the thumb, as the Stones once had it. In fact, this song is a direct role reversal of 'Under My Thumb', as it has a man reprimanded by his friends for being entirely dominated by his woman. Indeed, the lyric refers to the even blunter (if anatomically close) 'she's got you by the balls'. It's fun, but it is inessential and definite filler. Ian 'no minor chords' Stewart plays on this one as it is in his ballpark – indeed Richards has confirmed that Stewart only tended to play on the songs he liked, leaving the arguably far more talented Nicky Hopkins or Billy Preston to pick up the slack on the ones he didn't want, which seems an astonishingly arrogant attitude. Then again, the ones which didn't interest him often tended to be the better ones in any case, thus ensuring that Hopkins in particular enhanced his reputation enormously through his Stones work. And deservedly so.

'Fingerprint File' (Jagger, Richards)

The Stones get seriously funky! No soul, no blues, no rock, this is sheer, unadulterated funk, and it's a great example as well, for a band who have never dipped their toes anywhere near as far as this into the form. Jagger, Richards and Taylor all play guitar here, but there is no solo between them, only some occasional lead licks from, presumably, Taylor. Indeed, it is Taylor who also provides the hugely impressive bass on this one, bringing the funk from start to finish, especially when a partial breakdown brings the bassline front and centre. Wyman does appear, though unusually he is playing synthesizer. Hopkins and Preston provide piano and clavinet.

Lyrically, this is dark and oppressive, as Jagger seems to be inhabiting, or at least believing he inhabits, a totalitarian 1984 world of surveillance and 'Big Brother' tactics. It may not be entirely coincidental that this was written in 1973, the year of the Watergate scandal. As the song progresses, Jagger seems to get more secretive and mysterious, descending into partial covert-sounding spoken word, before ending with a climactic whispered 'Goodnight! Sleep tight!' which is quite chilling in the context of the song. An exceptional, if utterly atypical, way to end what is another hugely underrated album, along with *Goats Head Soup*. The writing off of these two albums after *Exile*, as happens very often, is quite baffling, as the musical growth the band present throughout is exceptional.

Next, however, was to be the arrival of Ron Wood, and the start of another era in the band's evolution with a very different style of musician from the departing Taylor.

Related Song:

'Through the Lonely Nights' (Jagger, Richards)

The B-side to the 'It's Only Rock 'n' Roll' single, this track was recorded during the *Goats Head Soup* sessions but held over for space reasons. It is another pleasant Stones ballad, with some nice Taylor lead guitar work, albeit a frustratingly brief solo. It isn't essential. It has always been strongly rumoured that Jimmy Page appears on this, but it has never been corroborated.

Black and Blue (1976)

Personnel:
Mick Jagger: vocals, guitar, piano
Keith Richards: guitar, vocals, bass, piano
Ron Wood: guitar, vocals
Bill Wyman: bass
Charlie Watts: drums and percussion
With
Nicky Hopkins: piano, organ, synthesizer
Billy Preston: piano, organ, synthesizer
Harvey Mandel: guitar
Wayne Perkins: guitar

Record Label: Rolling Stones Records
Recorded: December 1974-February 1976, produced by Jagger/Richards (credited as The Glimmer Twins)
Release Date: April 1976
Highest chart places: UK: 2, US: 1
Running time: 41:24

Album Facts:

After the release of *It's Only Rock 'n' Roll*, the band elected not to go out on the road to promote it, but instead to go straight back into the studio in December 1974 and begin work on the next album, much to the disagreement of Mick Taylor. Indeed, so strongly did the guitarist oppose this plan that he failed to show up for the sessions and instead tendered his resignation, prompting Jagger to claim later that he received two phone calls on the same day – the first to say that Taylor would not be attending the recording sessions and the second to say that he wouldn't be attending anything with the Stones from then on. The band did not go out on tour again until the 1975 'Tour of The Americas', by which time Ron Wood had joined and was playing in Taylor's place. A much more basic and unadorned guitarist than Taylor, and by extension certainly a weaker musician overall than Brian Jones before him, Ron Wood can be seen in some ways as a classic example of a personality fit as opposed to a purely musical choice. What he may have lacked in Taylor's musical chops, he more than made up for in his rock-and-roll lifestyle, onstage swagger and general 'rock star' air. He fitted in as a foil for Richards like the missing piece of a jigsaw, which may go quite some way to explaining why he is still there today. Put simply, Ron Wood was a Rolling Stone waiting to happen.

It wasn't as straightforward as that by a long way, however. When work started at the end of 1974 in Munich the Stones were a four-piece, with the addition of Nicky Hopkins, and began work as such. For further sessions in Rotterdam, before the 1975 American tour, guitarists Harvey Mandel and ex-Canned Heat man Wayne Perkins were playing with the band at differing times, with both tipped as permanent replacements at one time or another, particularly Perkins who was practically crowned as the new man by some of the music papers. Ron Wood finally met up with the band at the beginning of April and was told the same month that he would be the permanent new Stone. However, he was still officially contracted to The Faces, so he did the 1975 tour as a 'guest musician' as nobody was officially informed of his joining until December 1975, when Rod Stewart left The Faces and the cat could finally be let out of the bag. Among the others to audition were Steve Marriott and Peter Frampton, while both Jeff Beck and Rory Gallagher went in to jam with the band, though without either wishing to join.

As a result of all this, while *Black and Blue* is Wood's debut with the band, it is scarcely 'his' album, in the same way that Mick Taylor had only been partially represented on *Let It Bleed*. He only plays guitar on two (or possibly three) of the eight tracks, contributing backing vocals to some others, as Perkins and Mandel feature heavily.

Album Cover:

The album came as a gatefold vinyl, with a wraparound photo taken in Florida of the five members as headshots. Richards and Wood appear in profile at either end, with Watts joining Wood and a quarter of Jagger's head on the reverse half. The front has Richards appearing to speak into a disinterested looking Jagger's ear, while a shadowy and inscrutable Wyman lurks in the background, with a large pointed collar giving him the appearance of a vampire with a dramatic cape. Perhaps Keith is whispering 'Hey Mick, Wyman's turned up for the session this time', or perhaps more likely 'shall we let him play on this one?' – who can say? The inner gatefold showed all five of the band on a beach, making light patterns in the air, in a rather pointless waste of prime cover space, it has to be said. There was a lyric sheet with the album, as well as an inner sleeve bearing what purports to be handwritten studio notes depicting who played what and when. It is a mine of information, but even then it appears to be misleading in a few instances.

Even as they began moving into their thirty-something 'elder statesmen' role a little more, the Stones proved themselves still able to court controversy, as a promotional photo (used as a large billboard before it was forcibly removed) depicted a near-naked model named Anita Russell, straddling the album sleeve, made up to be severely bruised and with her hands tied above her head, and bore the legend 'I'm Black and Blue from the Rolling Stones, and I love it'. You can see in retrospect how that one was never going to fly. Still, at least it wasn't proposed as the album cover this time out. The image still appeared, minus the provocative lettering, as a full-page ad in the music press. How times change.

'Hot Stuff' (Jagger, Richards)

Continuing the funk from 'Fingerprint File', but this time in an unashamed disco direction, there is just enough of a rock feel to make this infectious number recognisably Stones. Holding down a repetitive funk rhythm, with Watts and Wyman keeping it pinned right down, the track makes for a good opener, even if it does run out of steam a minute or so short of its five-and-a-half-minute running time. Harvey Mandel is all over this, with some searing wah-wah drenched lead guitar work, soloing as if his life depends on it. The lyrics are unimportant, existing largely to support the keynote phrase 'Hot stuff, can't get enough', with vague waffling about music helping Jagger in both body and soul, etc. The voice is effectively an instrument here. For the extended closing section, delivered in a sort of 'dub' vocal style, Mick adopts his beloved cod-Jamaican accent again, but it's lower in the mix and he gets away with it this time out. An official promo video has the Stones playing the song apparently live, accompanied by fellow participants Billy Preston and percussionist Ollie Brown, but Ron Wood is shown playing Mandel's lead guitar parts. He is also smoking a cigarette as he plays, which Jagger playfully takes out of his mouth and smokes himself. Straight away, he clearly knew his role: Keith Number Two. Jagger apparently had the Ohio Players in mind as the template for this one, and that's not far off as a comparison.

'Hand of Fate' (Jagger, Richards)

In contrast to the opener, this cracking track is a straight-up rocker with a classic Jagger lyric telling the story of a man who has killed another in a fight over a woman ('he shot me once but I shot him twice') and has gone on the run with the 'hand of fate', or justice, hovering over him. It's pure Stones all the way, with Jagger and Richards written through the middle of it like a stick of Blackpool rock, but arguably the real honours here go to guitarist Wayne Perkins, who manages to take no less than three grandstanding guitar solos within the four-and-a-half minute song. An experienced player who had worked with everyone from Clapton to Bob Marley, his high-mixed, stinging lead guitar runs here are quite reminiscent of Taylor, and add a huge amount to an already excellent song. It can only be speculated what the band might have gone on to do had he been offered the job, and on this evidence, it is hard to argue that it would not have been for the greater good of the music. He might not have stayed around for four decades like Wood, but whatever tenure he did have would surely have produced some bottled lightning.

'Cherry Oh Baby' (Donaldson)

The original of this reggae song was by Eric Donaldson and was a hit in his native Jamaica in 1971. The Stones heard it soon afterwards and, four years later, had a crack at it themselves, 'for a laugh' as Jagger has said, and they kept it on the album. This was not a great decision, and much of the audience was most certainly not laughing. The band's first full excursion into reggae after they dipped their toes in the water with 'Luxury' is, put bluntly, hopeless. Watts is all over the place, with no clue how to accent the off-beat correctly, while the guitars are feeble and unconvincing. Hopkins' organ phrases are more suited to a fairground ride and Jagger – well, you know what he's going to sound like on this. Bill Wyman tries manfully to hold down the beat, but apart from that nobody escapes intact from this car crash. One of the real low points in the Stones career up to this point, it is the kind of track that the 'skip' button on a CD player was made for. They would get better at reggae later on in their careers, but at this point, and on this evidence, they simply weren't up to it. You really would think there would have been something better in reserve than this...

'Memory Motel' (Jagger, Richards)

Very close in spirit to 'Moonlight Mile', this wistful on-the-road song of lost love was begun by Jagger when the Stones were rehearsing at Andy Warhol's house in Montauk, Long Island, before the 1975 'Tour of The Americas'. There is, or was, an actual establishment called the Memory Motel nearby, and it is this which inspired the title, and the setting where the single night of romance takes place in the song. From this point, Jagger mentions leaving for Baton Rouge, which was indeed the location where the band played their first two warm-up shows for the tour once they left Montauk. He completed the lyric during the tour, in particular, the final verse relating to the dead-eyed travelling schedule and the tearful night of drunken memories he experiences. It's a fantastically emotive song, and there can be few serious listeners to the band who have not had a memory or two of their own conjured up by the chorus of 'You're just a memory / Of a love that meant so much to me'. Jagger wrote most of the song, but he was lacking a middle eight, so Keith provided one, and sings lead vocals on that section on the recording.

At seven minutes, it is long for a Stones track, but on this occasion, it is not padded out by any gratuitous soloing. Harvey Mandel provides some beautifully tasteful lead guitar work (Wayne Perkins is on acoustic guitar) but does not take any grandstanding solo part, instead working admirably in the service of the song. Interestingly, while Jagger and Richards are on the recording, they both provide just vocals and piano, Mick playing the intro with his first recorded keyboard part and Keith providing electric piano. Billy Preston plays synth, with some string-like effects.

It is unknown who the girl 'Hannah Honey' is based on – some have claimed Carly Simon, others the Stones tour photographer Annie Liebovitz (who did spend time with the band in Montauk), but Jagger has claimed that to his recollection it wasn't about any single girl or experience, but instead the whole tour and the nostalgia evoked by it. An excellent song, though.

'Hey Negrita' (Jagger, Richards)

This was, essentially, Ron Wood's song, though it is, as usual, credited to the Glimmer Twins. Wood allegedly turned up at rehearsal one day and announced he had something to play. He began the introductory riff, the band followed, and soon a song was born – providing Jagger with some more, slightly harsh, lyrical controversy. 'Negrita' was a term for a young black girl, and was also the nickname of his wife, Bianca, while the words deal with a man trying to get the price of a hooker negotiated down. There's nothing obscene in there though and, compared to 'Brown Sugar' and a few others, it's practically choirboy material! The words aren't really important in any case, more something to hang against the furiously gyratory beat. The track was very loose and unplanned, and a sort of jam for much of its length. Another which begins without much fanfare yet really seems to get cooking as it finds its feet. Wood at least got a credit for 'inspiration', which is better than nothing, while still not putting food on the metaphorical table.

There was a promo video for the song, with the band again playing live in the same large warehouse-looking location as the 'Hot Stuff' video. Jagger has a history of looking ridiculous in these things, but his bright green puff-sleeved outfit here, twinned with rainbow headband and absurd glasses takes some beating. The backside area of this ghastly ensemble, by the way, is silver. Which he uses to gesture to with all the subtlety of a flying mallet when he sings 'my sweet ass'. Honestly, if he'd just gone one step further and topped it off with a basket of fruit on his head, he could have gone to a fancy dress party as Carmen Miranda.

'Melody' (Jagger, Richards)

This time out Billy Preston is the man cast in the role of 'thanks for the song, we won't credit you, go away'. This distinctly jazzy piece first emerged from a melodic line by Preston, refined between him and Jagger, and like others before him, he fully expected a writing credit. According to Ron Wood, Preston 'took umbrage' at this, and considering how much the song clearly owes to him, it is unsurprising that he would not be best pleased. Again, the credit for 'inspiration' probably came as scant consolation.

The song itself is a cool, jazz tune perfectly suited to being played in some sort of night club in an old film noir movie, with the patrons sitting at small tables with lamps upon them, drinking martinis. Lyrically it concerns a woman who two-times the hapless narrator with his best friend before stealing a large proportion of his belongings and skipping town. He vows vengeance and pursues her relentlessly. The quite dramatic verses slip back each time into the repeated chorus line of 'Melody, it was her second name', which becomes quite hypnotic as the song goes on, even if it does push things slightly getting towards six minutes, with the last couple of those featuring Jagger's dreaded 'scat singing' and what can only be described as animal impersonations. He's good, but sometimes he needs to rein it in just a little. Oddly, we never find out what her first name is, but I imagine that 'Hilda, it was her first name' would have failed to have the same impact.

With Preston covering all of the keyboards and some vocals, the rest of the Stones are on their usual duty (except for the absent Wood), although Jagger not only being credited with 'foot stomp' but also having a full track on the recording devoted to this stomping seems a little unnecessary.

'Fool to Cry' (Jagger, Richards)

Another prime Stones ballad in the vein of 'Angie' and 'Wild Horses', this was the single release from the album and reached Number Six in the UK and Ten in the US. It begins with Jagger as a man who is tired after working all night, and when he returns home and puts his daughter on his knee, she tells him he is, as you might expect, a fool to cry. He is also told the same message by his friends and a lady in the poor part of town, with whom he is romantically linked – oddly, these people all call him 'daddy' as well, and we can only hope he isn't! The performance and delivery carry far more weight than the actual lyric in this one, without a doubt. Jagger plays electric piano throughout while Nicky Hopkins steps in with a superb turn on the regular piano. Wayne Perkins handles some beautiful lead guitar work while Wood is again absent.

'Crazy Mama' (Jagger, Richards)

The B-side to the 'Fool to Cry' single, this was a popular track among fans and critics alike. A quintessential chugging Stones rocker, it sees Jagger swearing vengeance on the crazy female of the title, who has apparently visited all manner of troubles on him, described as having a ball and chain and a sawn-off shotgun, as well as references to old-time religion, superstition and sacrifices, in a verse which sounds extremely voodoo-esque. This is all delivered by Mick in a manner which gives the impression of him being delighted to be let off the leash on a proper blood-and-thunder Stones charger after all of the funk, reggae, crooning and jazz which makes up so much of this extremely eclectic album. Jagger is also responsible for the rhythm guitar part which opens the song, while Keith takes care of most of the rest of the guitars, including the distinctive slide part, as well as the bass (no Wyman on here). While not credited as such, the lead guitar parts on the song sound very much more in Ron Wood's style than Keith's, so it may be that he is in the mix.

An excellent way to end a transitional yet interesting album, which was lauded and reviled in equal measures by the critics on release, with most ultimately settling for the middle ground: while it's not the band's greatest album, it is far from their worst either.

Some Girls (1978)

Personnel:
Mick Jagger: vocals, guitar, piano
Keith Richards: guitar, vocals, bass, piano
Ron Wood: guitar, bass, pedal steel guitar, vocals
Bill Wyman: bass, synthesizer
Charlie Watts: drums and percussion
With
Sugar Blue: harmonica
Ian McLagan: piano, organ
Mel Collins: Saxophone

Record Label: Rolling Stones Records
Recorded: October 1977-March 1978, produced by Jagger/Richards (credited as The Glimmer Twins)
Release Date: June 1978
Highest chart places: UK: 2, US: 1
Running time: 40:45

Album Facts:

For the first time since *Exile*, the band recorded an album in France – at the Pathé-Marconi EMI Studios near Paris. While the sessions ran from November '77 to March '78, it appears that almost all of the album was recorded before Christmas 1977, with only 'Before They Make Me Run' coming from the later recordings. Several more tracks recorded at those later sessions, however, which had been discarded, were finally issued on a bonus CD some three decades later.

The album was recorded under a very real threat to the band's future existence, with Keith Richards awaiting trial on drugs offences in Canada, which could easily have led to a lengthy prison sentence which, as Jagger admitted at the time, would almost certainly have led to the break-up of the band. The bust in question occurred in February 1977, where Keith and Anita were arrested in their hotel room by Mounted Police (that is to say, the Canadian Mounted Police, not that they were on their horses in the hotel!) for possession of heroin. They were suspected of trafficking, which was the offence which carried the danger of lengthy jail time. The trial did not take place for an absurdly lengthy nineteen months, but in that time Keith did receive permission to leave Canada for the US (thanks to then-President Jimmy Carter) in order to undergo detox treatment in New York, and he was also granted a working visa to allow him to travel to France for the recording sessions.

Strangely for an album recorded in France, the tracks are liberally sprinkled with references to New York. The release of the record came in an uncertain musical climate when the advent of the punk and new wave movement threatened to sweep away 'dinosaurs' such as the Stones and others of their vintage. Indeed, the Clash song '1977' actually declared 'No Elvis, Beatles or Rolling Stones in 1977' in its chorus. Triumphantly, however, *Some Girls* reached the top of the US charts (and second spot in the UK), indicating a staying power far beyond what their nay-sayers were predicting. Many still claim that it is 'the last great Rolling Stones album', though others go back half a decade earlier to *Exile on Main Street* for that claim. Relatively few cite any album after the '70s as a Stones classic on the level as these.

Album Cover:

Some things never changed, as the album cover once again brought with it lawsuits and banned images! This time around there were no toilet wall or zip fasteners to provoke hysterical indecency claims – on this occasion, it was something as innocuous as failure to agree on copyright permission which scuppered things. The basic premise of the cover was similar to that used by Led Zeppelin for their *Physical Graffiti* album, with die-cut holes in the outer sleeve having different images from the inner sleeve visible through them, but this cover (designed by Peter Corriston and illustrator Hubert Kretzschmar) had as its outer template a design based on an old advertisement for the Valmor Products corporation, featuring heads with various wigs on them in garishly coloured price bands. The faces were cut out and the inner sleeve featured a collage of various celebrities as well as the Stones themselves, with their faces fitting into the empty spaces. Unfortunately, no permission had been sought for the use of these likenesses, and the band were hit by threatened lawsuits from Lucille Ball, Farrah Fawcett, Raquel Welch, Liza Minnelli (on behalf of her mother Judy Garland) and the estate of Marilyn Monroe. A reworked sleeve was hastily issued, with these images withdrawn (plus others not yet complained about, including Brigitte Bardot, Jayne Mansfield, Gina Lollobrigida and Rita Hayworth – presumably as a pre-emptive safety measure) and replaced by crude coloured rectangles and the phrases 'Pardon our appearance' and 'Cover under reconstruction'. There was talk of a new, permanent, cover design to replace this, this time featuring female celebrities who had said they would like to be included, but this never happened and the temporary compromise sadly remained in place. Valmor Products, meanwhile, issued their own lawsuit but did not request the cover be changed – they simply settled quite wisely for a substantial amount of money and the continued publicity!

'Miss You' (Jagger, Richards)

A massive hit as a single, this track was inspired by the disco beat which the band, particularly Jagger, had been soaking up in New York's Studio 54 club. A divisive song among fans, it is unquestionably an excellent disco track and contains some brilliantly funky bass from Bill Wyman and some nice lead guitar work from Wood, but the question was whether people wanted an excellent disco track from the Rolling Stones. The answer from the worldwide general populace was a resounding 'yes' based on sales and chart positions, even if some of the die-hards would forever disagree. The harmonica on the track is provided by Sugar Blue (real name James Whiting), a native of Harlem who was actually discovered playing in the Paris subway while the band were recording.

There was an extended 12" single version of the song, running to over eight minutes, which really sounds as if it would become tiresome. However, surprisingly, this is more successful than the shorter album version as it not only features some excellent additional guitar work but also seems to absorb the listener more into the groove of the track. John Lennon claimed that 'Miss You' was largely a speeded-up take on his own track 'Bless You' from the *Walls and Bridges* album, but this seems somewhat of a stretch.

'When the Whip Comes Down' (Jagger, Richards)

From funk to punk, one might say! From the overt disco influence of 'Miss You', the band now immediately turn their attention towards the other prevailing music trend of the day, the punk/new wave scene, and immediately proceed to own it! This track is an absolute stormer – raw, aggressive, fast-paced and lyrically edgy. The song concerns an openly gay man from LA who travels to New York and gets himself a 'trade' – though one suspects this not to be that of a garbage collector, as Jagger tried to claim at the time. The blatant reference to 53rd Street (an area infamous for male prostitution at the time) gives a large hint as to how he might be earning his money. The chorus powers along with a couple of power chords perfectly set behind each line to impart the unstoppable forward momentum it thrives on, and the pace never lets up. The B-side of the single 'Respectable', this was one of the best Stones tracks for some considerable time. Wood handles the lead work; it's not exactly the work of a maestro, but that isn't the point with this one. It's all about that slashing rhythm guitar, provided by both Keith and Mick.

'Just My Imagination (Running Away with Me)' (Whitfield, Strong)

Once again, the Stones do the Temptations, just as they did with 'Ain't Too Proud to Beg' on the *It's Only Rock and Roll* album. This time out they actually do a pretty decent job, turning the breezy soul of the original into a fairly convincing mid-paced rock song. Wood contributes some decent, if fairly basic, soloing as he and Keith showcase their 'weaving' technique, where each fills the gaps left by the other. It's not going to win many 'best Stones track' polls, but it's an original twist on a well-known song which does its job well enough.

'Some Girls' (Jagger, Richards)

Here's Jagger proving that he can still offend people with his lyrics – in this case, women pretty much across the board are the direct hit as he issues every sort of stereotypical generalisation you could possibly imagine! Not content with this, our Mick manages to rope in the fury of the entire black population as well with the infamous line 'black girls want to get fucked all night', which had Ahmet Ertegun and Atlantic Records facing a deluge of complaints. For all of this, it's an enjoyable track musically in its own right, a loping country-tinged mid-paced rocker with a chorus that gains in infectiousness as the song develops.

There are echoes of Bob Dylan here: firstly, particularly on the line 'gave me a lethal dose', Jagger channel's Dylan's distinctive delivery very closely, while the 'I'll buy you a house back in Zuma Beach and give you half of what I own' references Dylan's divorce from wife Sara, who took the house they owned near Zuma Beach, Malibu in the settlement.

'Lies' (Jagger, Richards)

Here the Stones are clearly trying to prove to the New Wave that 'whatever they can do, we can do better'. From the fast, basic guitar-driven accompaniment to Jagger's sneering, faux-angry vocal, everything is tailored right to that exact template, with even the lyric carrying the nihilistic message that everybody lies. The trouble is, in trying so hard to sound young and vital and relevant, they inadvertently miss everything which gives them their genius. The guitars clatter along, with none of the Richards genius of things like 'Jumping Jack Flash' or 'Brown Sugar', the rhythm section pound gamely yet mechanically away and Jagger dumbs down his vocal as he tries to sound furious about these 'lies' that they told him, including the ghastly clichés of the teachers in school and his 'history books'. Coming from the man who made those very history books come alive in such magnificent fashion in 'Sympathy for the Devil', this is poor fare indeed. In trying to ape their younger peers, they merely come across as empty, like an embarrassing dad trying to dance with his kids. They roll along happily enough on this one, but without gathering any meaningful moss.

'Far Away Eyes' (Jagger, Richards)

Interestingly, Side Two of the album begins with a song which by its own success demonstrates exactly why 'Lies' failed – namely, a sense of humour. In this country pastiche, which is clearly hugely influenced by Gram Parsons, and songs such as 'Drug Store Truck-Drivin' Man', the band manage to play a lugubrious, loping country swing as well as anyone, while Ronnie Wood plays some excellent pedal steel guitar. Crucially, however, they aren't trying to beat the likes of Parsons and bands like Poco at their own game, and Jagger's half-spoken verses display a marvellous streak of sardonic humour which is pitched at the perfect level to puncture any pomposity the song may have had, and throws the harmonised chorus into sharp, and infectiously 'sing-able' relief. It's an affectionate parody, for sure, but it works perfectly. There is a promo video for the song, which is simply the band playing the song in a room, but Jagger's gurning self-deprecating delivery contrasting with the doleful expressions of the other four makes it tremendously enjoyable. The setting of Bakersfield is, of course, deliberate, as a reference to the so-called 'Bakersfield Sound' of the particular brand of modern country beloved of contemporary country-rock musicians. This was the B-side of the 'Miss You' single, which must have confused the hell out of a whole lot of teenage disco fans!

'Respectable' (Jagger, Richards)

Back to the punk thing again here, with this reasonable yet undistinguished rocker. A rather basic thrash, it was originally written in a slower tempo, but either Mick or Keith insisted it be sped up to fit with the prevailing trend (both have blamed the other!) – either way, this might have made it more commercial, but whether it was a valid artistic move is open to debate. The lyrics are interesting, in the sense that they can be taken either as a cynical take on how 'respectable' the band had become of late, or else a take on the relationship Jagger's wife Bianca allegedly had with the son of then-President Gerald Ford (references to 'heroin with the President' and 'the easiest lay on the White House lawn' certainly back this up, along with the line 'don't take my wife'). Unfortunately, such interesting, and possibly contentious, lyrics don't last too long as the song descends into endless chorus repetitions.

The promo video is faintly embarrassing, showing the band in 'young and edgy' attire and Jagger (resplendent in white Stones t-shirt) thrashing away at a Fender Jaguar guitar. Worst of all, midway through the song, Jagger uses said instrument to smash through the (paper) wall into another room, as the band all leap through after him and continue playing, as he himself descends into parodying the then in-vogue Bob Geldof. It's a long way from the Prince of Darkness strutting the stage at Altamont, that's for sure. The track was released as a single in the UK (with the far superior 'When the Whip Comes Down' on the flip), but it stalled at Number 23. Respectable? Perhaps. Irrelevant? Dangerously close...

'Before They Make Me Run' (Jagger, Richards)

Keith enters the limelight here for this track which does not even feature Jagger (apart from some backing vocals added later). Recorded over five days without sleep by a clearly wired and inspired Richards, this track is the first on the album to really hark back to the loose, slovenly feel of *Exile* and the like. Keith's lead vocal is thin and reedy, and the melody meanders a little, but, like *Exile* before it, somehow the track becomes much better than it really has any business being – showcasing along the way what that unique Stones 'fairy dust' was, and how it had been missing. The song clearly concern's Keith's upcoming Toronto drug trial which was looming over him, and this goes some way to explaining the earnestness captured in his less than technically great singing. He also handles bass duties in the absence of Wyman, and somehow manages to create a genuinely great Stones track out of very little. The working title of the song was 'Rotten Roll', incidentally.

'Beast of Burden' (Jagger, Richards)
This ode to a woman who is so adored by the narrator that he claims there is nothing he won't do to please her is another which was primarily the work of Richards before Jagger reworked some of the lyrics. It's an aching soul ballad, very much in the vein of the '60s sound of the likes of Al Green, and is pleasant if a little too much on the limp side. Jagger delivers the song with the right amount of tremulous emotion, the rhythm section are right on point and Wood plays some nice lead work, but the overall impression is a little half-hearted.

'Shattered' (Jagger, Richards)
The final track on the album is another one which takes inspiration from the new wave movement, but in this case the jerky, hyper-rhythmic new wave as played by the likes of XTC, Television and others, rather than the punk movement. The song is built around one big repetitive riff from Keith, played with significant phasing, while Jagger half-talks and half-sings the tale of seediness and urban decay in New York, using a vocal style often called Sprechgesang. There really isn't a lot going on beyond this, and it doesn't end the album on a particularly high note. Wood plays the bass (no Wyman again) and a rather dull solo, while backing vocals eagerly repeat the odd phrase 'Sha-ooby, shattered', which was apparently the last remnant of Keith's original lyric before Mick wrote the final take. Note that, in the line 'Schmatta, schmatta, schmatta, I can't give it away on Seventh Avenue', the word 'Schmatta' is Yiddish slang for ragged clothes and Seventh Avenue is the Manhattan fashion district.

Ultimately, it is another example of the band chasing the contemporary zeitgeist at a time in their careers when they should have been able to step out of that competitiveness and be true to themselves. Though much-praised, *Some Girls* does, in the final analysis, contain rather too much of that.

Related Song:

'Everything Is Turning to Gold' (Jagger, Richards, Wood)
This funky, horn-driven number was recorded during the sessions for the album but only saw the light of day as the B-side to 'Shattered' when it was released unsuccessfully as a single in the US. Credited to Wood in addition to the Twins, he claims that he actually wrote the majority of it, and the inspiration was the birth of his son Jesse. It moves along quite nicely, but it isn't particularly distinguished to be honest. The horns appearing mid-way through at first seem to beef up the power somewhat, but quickly become a little obtrusive. The track was included on the 1981 compilation album *Sucking In The Seventies*, one would assume as a quite blatant attempt to sell the album to those who didn't have the song, along with other previously rare or unreleased tracks used on it.

Emotional Rescue (1980)

Mick Jagger: vocals, guitar, piano
Keith Richards: guitar, vocals, bass, piano
Ron Wood: guitar, bass, pedal steel guitar, vocals
Bill Wyman: bass, synthesizer
Charlie Watts: drums and percussion
With
Nicky Hopkins: keyboards
Ian Stewart: piano
Bobby Keys: Saxophone
Sugar Blue: harmonica
Michael Shrieve: percussion

Record Label: Rolling Stones Records
Recorded: January-December 1979, produced by Jagger/Richards (credited as The Glimmer Twins)
Release Date: June 1980
Highest chart places: UK: 1, US: 1
Running time: 41:15

Album Facts:

For the follow-up to *Some Girls*, as soon as they came off the road promoting that album the Stones decamped to Compass Studios in the Bahamas to begin work on the follow-up. They were full of optimism and confidence after the success of the previous album, and especially so after Richards' court case finally ended with his acquittal on the proviso that he play two free charity concerts and continue with his free rehab treatment (the concerts were played on behalf of the blind at the Oshawa Civic Auditorium, both on 22 April 1979, by Keith and Ronnie's band The New Barbarians). According to Richards, the judge concluded with 'I will not incarcerate him for addiction and wealth'. Everything seemed rosy in the Stones' garden and continued in that vein when they moved to their favoured Pathé-Marconi studios in France in the latter half of the year. However, things behind the scenes were not quite so idyllic with, Bill Wyman remembers, tension, frustration, health problems and constant lateness bedevilling the sessions. By the time the album was being mixed early the following year, Wyman recalls Richards accusing Jagger of 'listening to too many bad records' and trying to calculate the market, while Keith simply wanted to make a good rock and roll record.

When the album appeared in April 1980, it made the top of the charts on both sides of the Atlantic, but this was largely on the back of the much-praised *Some Girls*, and reviews were not generally positive. Over the years, the album's reputation has not worn particularly well and it is often cited as the moment when the wheels really began to come loose.

Album Cover:

Put simply, the cover design was a disaster. The front and back covers of the non-gatefold sleeve were adorned with nothing except dull, monochrome shots of the band members, taken with a thermal imaging camera and therefore completely unrecognisable. There were four on the front and a collage of smaller ones on the back. It was a little like looking at a pile of X-rays. There was a poster with the album, which features – yes – more thermal imaging camera shots, this time in colour but scarcely more interesting. Basic album credits were included on the back. The record company shipped large displays of the cover to record shops to be prominently displayed in their windows, to an enormous shrug of the shoulders from an unimpressed public. This time around nobody would be offended or litigious as a result of the cover. Essentially because nobody cared enough about it. The band had produced some less than sterling cover designs before (let's face it, *Let It Bleed* and *Black and Blue* had been pretty uninspired) but this was easily the worst yet.

'Dance (Pt.1)' (Jagger, Richards, Wood)

The title of this opening cut hardly fills the traditional Stones fan with confidence, and indeed this trepidation is not misplaced. The track takes the template of 'Miss You' and runs with it way too far. The funky bass of Wyman is again excellent, and the band's ability to play disco music cannot be faulted, but this really wasn't what most fans wanted. In fact, the end result wasn't what Keith wanted either, as he had originally conceived the track with Wood as an instrumental opener, but Jagger had insisted on adding vocals, much to his guitarist's disgust. Indeed, Richards' claim that the vocals 'totally nullified the track' have some credence, as they do appear like an irrelevant and totally inappropriate layer added to the top of the cake, and the track improves after the vocals finish and it is allowed to breathe a little. Bobby Keys was back in the fold on sax, but nobody really noticed. The compilation *Sucking In The Seventies* would later try to tempt fans in with an unreleased mix of the song called 'If I Was A Dancer (Dance Pt.2)', which is as interesting as you think it is going to be...

'Summer Romance' (Jagger, Richards)

Another title to conjure with from this sadly neutered version of the 'most dangerous band in the world', the lyrical content lives down to expectations as it concerns an affair between an adult and a high school student coming to a close with the end of summer. The depth of the song goes no deeper than the fact that she will be back in class and 'in the gym' while he will be 'in the pub, playing pool and drinking'. It is never revealed what the couple's relative ages are, but it doesn't evoke very salubrious imagery, let's just say that. Musically it is safe, sanitised sub-Chuck Berry rock and roll. Earlier takes were faster and more aggressive, but while that may be an improvement it isn't enough to save the song. Ian Stewart is on piano here, but once again nobody cared. Bill

Wyman avoided association with this hopeless effort by virtue of being absent from the studio and leaving the bass to Wood.

'Send It to Me' (Jagger, Richards)

More funk here, in tandem with reggae – a medium at which the Stones have regularly fallen flat on their faces. This isn't quite as bad as 'Cherry Oh Baby' for example, but it's far from great. Jagger appeals for everything from loving and money to, ultimately, what appears to be a wish for a mail order bride to be sent to him. He writes a lot of letters. And that's it. Nicky Hopkins becomes the latest ex-sideman to make a return in unflattering circumstances as the record continues to lurch from one failure to another. Surely things have to improve?

'Let Me Go' (Jagger, Richards)

At last, things look up a little with this entertaining rocker that sees, at last, some prime Jagger lyrics. He is at his cynical, dark-humoured best here as a man trying desperately to get out of an affair which has long turned toxic. 'Can't you get it through your thick head', he wails, 'this affair is finished dead!', and even better, 'So you think I'm giving you the brush off? Well, I'm just telling you to shove off'. From this, he goes as far as to contemplate hanging around in gay bars as a more pleasurable alternative. It's genuinely funny, utterly disrespectful and, at last, a proper Stones song. It's not exactly 'Street Fighting Man', but in this company, it's a beacon.

'Indian Girl' (Jagger, Richards)

With a few exceptions, the Stones have tended to shy away from overt political commentary, but here they look directly at the situation in war-torn Central America. Clearly influenced by Jagger's travels with Bianca, this song is set in her native Nicaragua (specifically Masaya), but also references other conflicts in the region. The 'Indian Girl' of the title has seen her father murdered and her mother raped, and the lyric is certainly one which pulls no punches. Musically, oddly enough, it retains the country flavour that the band have often used, with Ron Wood on his favoured pedal steel guitar, which seems somewhat incongruous with the subject matter. As a result, the track does not have the emotional impact it perhaps should have and seems to meander a little over its six minutes plus length. A shame, as it is a genuine attempt to lend some gravitas to the record, but it could have been done much more effectively.

'Where the Boys Go' (Jagger, Richards)

Now, what were we saying about gravitas and lyrical weight? You won't find it here. A vacuous composition about going out on a Saturday night and getting drunk, this is the nadir of the Stones' attempts to do 'punk', as they sound utterly ridiculous trying to appear like a bunch of 20-year-olds. The vocals are shouted out gormlessly in a fashion more associated with Sham 69 or the Cockney Rejects, and the whole thing is an embarrassment as the band desperately try to sound like people who were barely born when they had their first hits. The subject matter, banal though it is, can be done well – see Elton John's 'Saturday Night's All Right for Fighting', for example. Let us draw a veil over this disaster and move on.

'Down in The Hole' (Jagger, Richards)

Surprisingly, we are now back to the blues. And how! Almost as if realising the embarrassment of the previous track, the Stones return to the form of which they are masters, and they sound as if they've never been away. Jagger howls with despairing anguish as he appears to be addressing someone stripped of all their wealth in a sort of 'Like A Rolling Stone' manner, and he has rarely sounded better. Keith and Ronnie put in some superlative rhythm and lead work between them, trading lead lines to perfection. Sugar Blue returns with some searing harmonica, and the result is a four-minute track which one feels could have gone on for twice as long without outstaying its welcome. They could still do it when they wanted – they just didn't seem to want it often enough by this time. Easily the best track on the album.

'Emotional Rescue' (Jagger, Richards)

From the sublime to the faintly ridiculous. This disco/funk track is clearly cut from the same cloth as 'Miss You' (and released as a single likewise, in a clearly overt attempt to get a hit), but with one big difference – Jagger's vocal. Throughout the track, he adopts an absurdly exaggerated falsetto which reminds one of an even higher Bee Gees. It's an impressive display of vocal range as a technical exercise, but as a delivery of the song it is distracting to say the least. Bobby Keys, when he became one of the first to hear the final vocal, commented that he thought it was a joke 'when Jagger put that Minnie Mouse vocal on it'. It's a harsh assessment, but sadly accurate. The lyrics tell the tale of a girl, the object of the singer's desires, who lives with a rich man as his 'plaything', and his intentions to rescue her. It's not all that important as the words are largely inaudible as delivered in the aforementioned squeaky tone. Wood plays bass for some reason, despite Wyman's clear adeptness at a funky bassline – all the more strange as Wyman was actually present at the sessions, where he played a synthesizer part on the track. It was a sizeable hit but, once again, somewhat embarrassing for a band, and singer, whose 'name was called Disturbance' a decade earlier. It's a Jagger song, so Keith at least escapes with some credibility intact.

'She's So Cold' (Jagger, Richards)

Another jagged, poppy new-wave number here, again recalling the contemporaneous work of the Boomtown Rats, and once again the record's flaws are laid bare. Put simply, so little on this album sounds genuine, with track after track showing the one-time ploughers of their own dissolute furrow chasing the trends of the time like an eager puppy running after a ball. It's not an edifying spectacle, frankly, and the lyrical content here, with Jagger being 'so hot' for a girl who is 'so cold' is disposable at best, full of predictable references to volcanoes, ice cream cones and tombstones. Again, the clearly hit-obsessed Jagger is the driving force here, with the rest of the band depressingly willing to follow. One more track to come on the album: could it be hoped for a late improvement?

'All About You' (Jagger, Richards)

And, as if by magic, here comes good old Keith to the (non-emotional) rescue, as he delivers this excellent album closer, on which Jagger, significantly, does not even appear. Written around the time he was coming off heroin, the world-weariness in Richards' voice cannot be escaped on this bluesy, jazzy ballad which conjures up the feeling of coming down from a two-day 'bender' at 4 am. 'Tired' doesn't begin to describe it.

Lyrically, it is sardonic and cynical to the point of viciousness, with Jagger the main target of his frustration and resignation ('If the show must go on, let it go on without you / So sick of hanging around with jerks like you'), but also Anita Pallenberg, and their crumbling relationship. While recording the album, Scott Cantrell, Richards' gardener, was found dead in Anita's bed after, apparently, playing Russian roulette with Keith's Smith & Wesson gun. This event appears to be alluded to also in the ball of empty-eyed recrimination which makes up the lyric. He would be said to be baring his soul, if it did not sound as if he has no soul left to bare. It's an astonishing way to round out the band's second decade and stands out from most of the rest of the album like heroin from strawberries. Keith wouldn't have it any other way.

Live Albums and Compilations

Live Albums:

During the scope of this book, there were only three official Rolling Stones live recordings, and the first of these was never released in the UK. *Got Live If You Want It!* came out in the US in 1966 (following an EP of the same name in the band's home country), and was promptly disowned by the band, who consistently went on to claim that 1969's *Get Yer Ya-Ya's Out!* was their live album debut proper. At first glance, it is easy to understand these feelings as there is a lot of audience noise (the shows were in the UK in 1966) and in fact two of the tracks, 'I've Been Loving You Too Long' and 'Fortune Teller', weren't even live at all. In fact, they were studio versions with audience noise added to pad out the album, which gives it an air of questionable authenticity all round. However, most of the other ten tracks actually come over with a tremendous sense of power and excitement.

Crackling with electricity and adrenalin, songs like 'Under My Thumb', 'Get Off of My Cloud', 'The Last Time', 'Have You Seen Your Mother Baby' and '19th Nervous Breakdown' surpass the tempo and volume of the originals as they are hurled at the audience like three-minute incendiary devices. To break things up there is even an unexpected rendition of 'Lady Jane'. It's an album much better than its reputation, and the recommendation of its creators would have you believe.

Coming up three years later, in 1970, was an entirely different live beast altogether. The oddly titled *Get Yer Ya-Ya's Out!* (including the irritating superfluous apostrophe!) was recorded on the band's 1969 American tour, a week before the fateful Altamont show, and catches the band at the height of their Mephistophelean powers. The title actually comes from an old Blind Boy Fuller song called 'Get Yer Yas Yas Out', and it is, in fact, a sexual innuendo, with 'Ya-Yas' being a slang term for women's breasts. This is subtly illustrated in the bizarre cover photo, showing a leaping Charlie Watts resplendent in white trousers and T-shirt depicting a pair of said breasts, and also wearing a Stars-And-Stripes top hat. According to Watts, he often wore the 'breasts' shirt as stage gear while the hat was one of Jagger's favoured pieces of stage attire. He is holding two guitars, one in each hand, above his head, while at his side trudges a doleful looking donkey carrying a pair of drums and another guitar. It is surreal!

Musically the album showcases a band far removed from the powerful yet relatively simplistic band of the previous live album. With Mick Taylor on his first tour with the band, the album is full of top-class renditions of some of the band's greatest late '60s works, from the opening 'Jumpin' Jack Flash' to the riotous closing 'Street Fighting Man'. A highlight is an amped-up version of 'Sympathy for the Devil', which complements rather than dethrones the very different studio version, but the centrepiece is undoubtedly the nine-minute performance of 'Midnight Rambler' from the not-quite-released *Let It Bleed*. Jagger maintains an uncanny hold over the crowd as he manages to inhabit the central killer character to unsettling effect, alternately cajoling, pleading, threatening and bellowing. It's astonishing as it manages to eclipse a studio rendition which was still a week away from release! The whole band are on top form, with Mick Taylor immediately making his presence felt. The tour would mark the last one on which the core band (plus Ian Stewart) would perform without any guest musicians, and it was also the last Stones album released on Decca before the set-up of Rolling Stones Records. There were even nods back to the band's Chuck Berry roots with 'Carol' and 'Little Queenie'. Timeless indeed.

Fast forward now to 1977 for the release of the double live album *Love You Live*, recorded in 1975 and '76, which managed to polarise fans and critics alike. Some claimed the album was a shoddily performed mess which only indicated how far the band had fallen, while others praised the looseness of the band's sound and declared it to be an essential live document. As is so often the case with such things, the truth lies somewhere in between. For most of this hit-laden album, the band are on perfectly acceptable form, but it has to be said that the biggest let-down throughout is Jagger. He sounds oddly disconnected and almost disinterested at times, and his delivery of the lyrics – particularly on 'Honky Tonk Women' and 'Jumpin' Jack Flash' – is lazy in the extreme, serving as a distraction from the otherwise sound performances, rather than the focal point that he should be.

Three of the four sides of vinyl were made up of tracks across the back catalogue, mostly only as far back as 1968, but the remaining side consisted of four tracks recorded at an intimate show at the El Mocambo Club in Toronto for which the band went back to their blues and R&B roots. This side was claimed by many to be easily the most successful, while others criticised it saying that, while the performances were good, the material was not what they preferred. They couldn't always get what they wanted, you might say...

The remaining sides mostly concentrated on hits, although 'Fingerprint File', 'Hot Stuff' and 'Star Star' were a little more unexpected. The medley of 'If You Can't Rock Me' and 'Get Off of My Cloud' is the only appearance of a track dating from earlier than 1968, apart from the Toronto side. 'Sympathy for the Devil' is effective but pales next to the *Ya-Ya's* rendition, while 'Tumbling Dice' is hopelessly limp. Over four minutes of 'You Gotta Move' seems interminable, and one wonders why on earth it was included. Probably the most successful track on the album is 'You Can't Always Get What You Want', which is close to definitive. The album cover, designed by Andy Warhol and depicting a drawing of Jagger biting someone's hand ('biting the hand that feeds', perhaps), is a shoddy mess which should never have got past the design stage.

In recent years there have been a number of 'archive releases' of vintage shows from the '70s in particular, which generally bear out the accepted vision that Stones shows of the time were a very hit and miss affair – brilliance could be followed by a sloppy mess, often during the same show.

Compilations:

The path of Rolling Stones compilation albums between their inception and 1980 is a labyrinthine one, to say the least – and that is largely due to Decca who, after losing the band to their own eponymous label, embarked on one of the most lunatic repackaging schemes ever conceived.

Let's start at the beginning though, while the Stones were still with Decca and their first 'Greatest Hits' compilation was released in 1966. Titled *Big Hits (High Tide and Green Grass)*, it wasn't as simple as that since the two albums of that same name in the UK and US were released 8 months apart and had only seven tracks in common, as well as completely different cover art. When the UK version followed the US March '66 release in November of that year, by which time there had been two more hit singles, one does wonder why on earth they used the same title. Anyhow, the British album is the better representation, having two extra tracks and several key songs which the US version (despite the excellent inclusion of 'Play with Fire') lacks.

Moving on three years to 1969, following the departure of Jones, the follow-up *Through the Past Darkly*, appeared on both sides of the Atlantic, with the same cover artwork this time out. Things still weren't simple, however, as the US version had to include the tracks it had missed out with the early release of the previous compilation while the British release contained a track from the US album *Flowers*, a compilation of unreleased tracks and some which had appeared on UK-only albums. Still with me? Well, hold on as the ride gets bumpy...

Following the band's 'defection' to their own Rolling Stones Records label with *Sticky Fingers*, previous UK label Decca appeared to become extremely bitter at this development and lost all semblance of quality control and logic. As discussed elsewhere, the first rehashed product to be churned out was the album *Stone Age* in 1971, wrapping a bunch of older cuts which had not appeared on UK albums in a low-budget sleeve which lifted the banned (by Decca that is) *Beggars Banquet* graffiti art. The Stones were not amused and told everyone not to buy it. Falling over themselves in their rush to empty the pockets of the band's loyal fanbase, they followed this up later that same year with an album called *Gimme Shelter*, which trumpeted about unreleased live tracks and appeared to be related to the movie of the same name. In actual fact it had no connection to the film and consisted of one side of hits and another side containing half of the *Got Live If You Want It* album. They even had to apologise for that one, so misleading was it.

Still, not ones to be put off by a bit of admitted false advertising, Decca rumbled on into 1972 with another pointless release. Having seen the hugely popular US two-disc compilation album on London records in 1971 entitled *Hot Rocks 1964-1971* (a comprehensive round-up), they elected to put out *Milestones* (which was neither comprehensive nor a milestone), another single disc featuring some more rehashed random old tracks, all bundled in a hideous sleeve featuring a ghastly Jagger photo. Still in 1972, they followed this up swiftly with the similarly useless *Rock and Rolling Stones*, consisting of mostly R&B cover songs with '19th Nervous Breakdown' thrown into the mix as if by some madman. The cover this time consisted, for some reason best known to themselves, of Mick Jagger's head surrounded by a circular collage of motorcycles. You couldn't make this up.

In that same year, London Records in the US seemed to take some inspiration from this by releasing another double album *More Hot Rocks (Big Hits and Fazed Cookies)*, which by the nature of it being everything which didn't make the first *Hot Rocks*, contained virtually no Big Hits. This idea seemed to give Decca a new surge of inspiration, as they set about releasing an album of B-sides. When it appeared, it was reasonably entitled *No Stone Unturned*, but in fact, by now it had been watered down to such an extent that only eight of the twelve songs were B-sides. The cover attempted some creativity by portraying the band in devilishly wicked mode, although their chosen photograph of Brian Jones creeping around wielding a tiny garden fork and a nice glass of red wine did not really conjure up images of the Princes of Darkness.

An official compilation followed this, with the worthy third round up *Made in the Shade* appearing on the band's own label in 1975. Another horror was in the wings though, as Allen Klein's ABCKO label put out a complete mish-mash entitled *Metamorphosis* the same year. Originally conceived as an interesting trawl through unreleased material entitled, cheerfully, 'Necrophilia', and curated by Bill Wyman, that project had been dropped some time ago and replaced by what was half-filled by tracks not even recorded by the band, but instead recordings of songs intended for other artists with only Jagger's voice dubbed on. There were a few actual Stones tracks, mostly discussed elsewhere, but nothing was essential. The cover had the band with giant insect heads peeping out from behind masks of their own faces. Of course, it did.

More worthwhile product next, mercifully, as 1975 saw Decca get their act together and release a genuinely well compiled double album entitled *Rolled Gold*, which itself was shadowed by a TV-advertised double called *Get Stoned*, on the budget Arcade label, which actually slightly improved on the Decca track selection, somehow managing to license two tracks from *Sticky Fingers*. An official Rolling Stones Records collection from 1979 entitled *Time Waits For No One* proved to be an interesting compilation of '70s material mostly featuring album tracks rather than obvious singles.

Perhaps stung by their best effort being outdone by a budget label, 1980 saw one last hopeless swing-and-miss by Decca, who put out *Solid Rock*, another utterly pointless random collection of '60s material packaged in a sleeve showing the band carved from rock which was so poorly executed it made the somewhat similar *Deep Purple In Rock* appear to be vying for a place in the National Gallery. Decca would, mercifully, call it a day after one final roll of the non-tumbling dice in 1981 with *Slow Rollers*, a compilation album of Stones ballads which, true to form, were not all ballads.

The Decca compilation album series. Not sadly missed.

Epilogue – What Came Next

There was definitely a sense with *Emotional Rescue* that the Stones' peak years as leaders rather than followers were behind them, and for the most part that was the case. The next album, *Tattoo You*, consisted of holdovers from previous album sessions (albeit some of good quality, notably including 'Start Me Up'). Meanwhile, the 1982 series of big UK outdoor shows presented audiences with the less than edifying spectacle of Jagger resplendent in multicoloured exercise gear, including kneepads. Not to criticise his fitness regime, which has served him more than admirably, but this particular wardrobe choice made him appear as if he was about to lead some ghastly breakfast television exercise demonstration. Altamont seemed long, long ago.

After 1983's weak effort *Undercover*, a true nadir was plumbed with the dreadful *Dirty Work* from 1986, with both of these albums encased in the sort of hideous day-glo artwork which could only come from the '80s. There were better albums to come – 1989's *Steel Wheels* was full of merit and spawned an excellent world tour which harked back to their best live work. Releases since this have become sparse, although *Voodoo Lounge* from 1994 and *Bridges to Babylon* from 1997 both contained flashes of brilliance among bouts of filler, while 2005's *A Bigger Bang* (the most recent collection of original material to date) was a solid effort.

Effectively, from the advent of the 1980s on, the Rolling Stones appeared to accept that their place in the rock and roll pantheon had changed. No longer the dangerous band of exiles from previous decades, they settled into a sequence of enormous arena tours, with slick production values, extensive rehearsals and an array of backing musician and singers ensuring everything looked and sounded great, if perhaps just missing that edge which once made them so thrilling. Their albums were reasonably received and all sold well but were never the 'events' which the earlier albums, up to and including *Black and Blue*, had always been.

They had become, and still remain, elder statesmen of rock. Much welcomed, always entertaining, but still giving off the faintest sense of having become the band they never wanted to grow up to be. Even Keith Richards has been relatively clean and sober for some considerable time, although since around 1980 he has appeared to be living in a state of having been dead for a year, exhumed and embalmed. With Jagger long since having evolved into the consummate musician-cum-businessman, Watts still appearing bored with the whole thing and Wyman long since departed (he left the band in the 1990s), Keith is the sole person still embodying that long-ago spirit of the Stones. Since Lemmy passed away, the feeling grows ever stronger that he is the single most indestructible man in the business, and the one who most bleeds rock and roll. Let it bleed, Keith. Let it bleed.

Afterword – The Ultimate Playlist

Finally, and just to close things, here is a suggested 30-track playlist of the greatest Stones material from the period covered in this book. Purely the author's opinion, of course!

Play with Fire
Satisfaction
Get Off of My Cloud
19th Nervous Breakdown
Out of Time
Who's Been Sleeping Here
Paint It Black
Citadel
2000 Light Years from Home
Ruby Tuesday
Jumpin' Jack Flash
Sympathy for the Devil
Jigsaw Puzzle
Salt of the Earth
Street Fighting Man
Gimme Shelter
Brown Sugar
Sister Morphine
Wild Horses
Moonlight Mile
Tumblin' Dice
Ventilator Blues
100 Years Ago
Winter
Star Star
Time Waits For No One
Hand of Fate
Memory Motel
When the Whip Comes Down
Far Away Eyes

Bibliography

Carr, R., *The Rolling Stones: An Illustrated Record* (New English Library, 1976)

Richards, K., *Life* (W&N, 2010)

Wyman, B., *Rolling With The Stones* (DK, 2002)

Wyman, B., *Stone Alone* (Viking, 1990)

Norman, P., *Mick Jagger* (Harper, 2013)

Margotin P. and Guesdon J., *The Rolling Stones: All The Songs* (Black Dog & Leventhal, 2016)

Charone, B., Fielder, H. And Goldman V., *Through The Past Darkly* (Sounds Magazine two-part feature, 1976)

Booth, S. *The True Adventures Of The Rolling Stones* (Sphere, 1984)

Dawson J., *And On Piano ... Nicky Hopkins* (Desert Hearts, 2011)

Also from Sonicbond Publishing

On Track series

Queen Andrew Wild 978-1-78952-003-3

Emerson Lake and Palmer Mike Goode 978-1-78952-000-2

Deep Purple and Rainbow 1968-79 Steve Pilkington 978-1-78952-002-6

Yes Stephen Lambe 978-1-78952-001-9

Blue Oyster Cult Jacob Holm-Lupo 978-1-78952-007-1

The Beatles Andrew Wild 978-1-78952-009-5

Roy Wood and the Move James R Turner 978-1-78952-008-8

Genesis Stuart MacFarlane 978-1-78952-005-7

Jethro Tull Jordan Blum 978-1-78952-016-3

The Rolling Stones 1963-80 Steve Pilkington 978-1-78952-017-0

Judas Priest John Tucker 978-1-78952-018-7

Toto Jacob Holm-Lupo 978-1-78952-019-4

Van Der Graaf Generator Dan Coffey 978-1-78952-031-6

Frank Zappa 1966 to 1979 Eric Benac 978-1-78952-033-0

Elton John in the 1970s Peter Kearns 978-1-78952-034-7

The Moody Blues Geoffrey Feakes 978-1-78952-042-2

The Beatles Solo 1969-1980 Andrew Wild 978-1-78952-042-2

Steely Dan Jez Rowden 978-1-78952-043-9

On Screen series

Carry On… Stephen Lambe 978-1-78952-004-0

Audrey Hepburn Ellen Cheshire 978-1-78952-011-8

Powell and Pressburger Sam Proctor 978-1-78952-013-2

Seinfeld Seasons 1 to 5 Stephen Lambe 978-1-78952-012-5

Francis Ford Coppola Stephen Lambe 978-1-78952-022-4

Other Books

Not As Good As The Book Andy Tillison 978-1-78952-021-7

The Voice. Frank Sinatra in the 1940s

Stephen Lambe 978-1-78952-032-3

and many more to come!

Would you like to write for Sonicbond Publishing?

At Sonicbond Publishing we are always on the look-out for authors, particularly for our two main series:

On Track. Mixing fact with in depth analysis, the On Track series examines the work of a particular musical artist or group. All genres are considered from easy listening and jazz to 60s soul to 90s pop, via rock and metal.

On Screen. This series looks at the world of film and television. Subjects considered include directors, actors and writers, as well as entire television and film series. As with the On Track series, we balance fact with analysis.

While professional writing experience would, of course, be an advantage the most important qualification is to have real enthusiasm and knowledge of your subject. First-time authors are welcomed, but the ability to write well in English is essential.

Sonicbond Publishing has distribution throughout Europe and North America, and all books are also published in E-book form. Authors will be paid a royalty based on sales of their book.

Further details are available from www.sonicbondpublishing.co.uk. To contact us, complete the contact form there or email info@sonicbondpublishing.co.uk